The Angel of Bang Kwang Prison

The Angel of Bang Kwang Prison

by Susan Aldous

Published by Maverick House, Main Street, Dunshaughlin, Co. Meath, Ireland.
Maverick House Asia, Level 41, 323 United Centre Building, Silom Road, Bangrak, Bangkok 10500, Thailand.

www.maverickhouse.com
email: info@maverickhouse.com

ISBN 978-1-905379-32-3

Printed and bound by CPD.

5 4 3 2 1

The paper used in this book comes from wood pulp of managed forests. For every tree felled at least one tree is planted, thereby renewing natural resources.

ACKNOWLEDGEMENTS

After you have been kind, after love has stolen forth into the world and done its beautiful work, go back into the shadows again and say nothing!

It is with a grateful heart that I wish to acknowledge the numerous souls who have helped me to live my dreams, especially those who saw beyond a distraught teenager's hard exterior; their care, respect, prayers and support have been invaluable as they set me on a path to many wondrous adventures.

Thank you to my parents, who have always stood by me, allowing me plenty of encouragement to be the person that I was destined to be. It has been a daunting journey, yet you held fast with great faith. My sister, Annabel, thanks for being you and doing so with grace.

All at Maverick House; John Mooney, Jean Harrington, Adam Hyland, Gert Ackermann, and Sarah Ormston—you have been superb. Thank you for opening the challenging door to write this book, for your genuine respect and patience. Permitting me plenty of wriggle room was a gift indeed. I love that you see the importance of each life you publish.

Special credit, along with hugs and kisses, needs to be given to two incredibly gifted folk; Pornchai Sereemongkonpol and Nicola Pierce, without whom, my story would have remained locked away in my head. They diligently and lovingly worked their magic while wading through prisons, piles of paperwork, shelters, hours of tapes, embracing excursions to the middle of nowhere to meet with a solitary inmate, analysing endless emails, letters, documents, and articles, and all the while doing so with great respect and concern. I cannot thank you both enough.

Aree, Peter, Anne, and Tom my fellow warriors, thanks for contributing to this book by freely sharing your stories where ours met. Your willingness to regurgitate difficult times with sincere honesty is highly commendable, as are your accomplishments. You and all the families who trudged, cried and laughed with me are the real angels.

Thanks to the handful of lovely women who are my dearest friends. You come from far and near; Australia, Norway, North America and Thailand. You will catch glimpses of yourselves throughout this book; you have made so much of it possible with your support, kindness and wonderful women's caring intuition.

To my guy friends too, love you all, you treat me like a lady and once in a while, let me be one of the boys ... your insight, support and presence throughout many projects have always been particularly reassuring especially when it comes to dealing with heartbreaking situations.

To my crusading media compadres who have been brilliant throughout the years, thanks for taking up the cause and helping bring about change. Lives go on for the better because of your due diligence.

Muchas gracias, wonderful ones in Monterey and Santa Monica, you helped me keep spirit in body, head in place and heart beating, and still do in so many ways. True friends come in when the rest of the world go out! You are true friends forever! Hey Kenny Khan, here's looking at you Carney Kid! Can you believe it? We did it! Deidre, appreciate you girlfrien'!

To those who hold this book in your hands, thank you for choosing to read it. I pray that something, somewhere amongst the jumble of my life encourages you and makes you believe that you too can inspire another life for the better. I mean to say, if I can do it, so can you!

Lastly and most importantly, I wish to express gratitude to those who have and still do suffer in the darkness under the weight of unjust systems and indifference. To you who wait for the light to come; this book is to your credit—you are my teachers, my heroes, my friends, deeply affecting me to the innermost parts of my being through your bravery. By allowing me precious opportunities to reach out to you, true purpose and great beauty has been born into my world. I went to bring change to you, but you changed me, and it is through those changes I have found my life, my love and my work. You humble me.

With that said, I go back into the shadows.

DEDICATION

I'd like to dedicate this book to my beautiful daughter Talya.

You are such a meaningful part of my life. The journey would be incomplete without you; it would indeed be as if some great gift of love were missing.

Heaven only knows why you chose to come to earth via me, but I am extremely glad that you did. What a privilege to experience the depth of mother love by caring so deeply for you.

You are the uniqueness of pure originality, the heart of creativity, the soul of sensitivity, the prize of serendipity and hey, your humour rocks! I love you and am proud of you in ways that cannot be measured.

> Sophisticated, worldly-wise,
> I searched for God & found Him not,
> Until one day, the world forgot,
> I found Him in my baby's eyes.
> —Mary Afton Thacker

FOREWORD

As with many true stories, there are just too many personal experiences and important people who have come in and out of the writer's life to be able to recount them all.

My memoirs are such, and I have only been able to touch on a few of the many thousands of encounters, and relate to you the reader, a meagre unfolding of but a few lives. There are many more folk whose stories are equally significant or profound; some I have deliberately kept for another day for the simple reasons that they are too sacred or difficult to share at present. Some are not my stories to tell, or by so doing it would be inappropriate to divulge such intimacies of another's life. Additionally, in a number of cases, I have changed names and details so as to not reveal identities, endanger or cause discomfort to them or the organisations/ agencies that they are affiliated with.

In sharing my life, I have tried with the utmost conscientiousness to show humaneness and vulnerability in order to set to naught the erroneous beliefs that some folk have regarding volunteers. No, we are not saints, just ordinary people, fighting everyday problems while trying to make a difference. All I ask for is that you the reader allow me one thing. I am hopelessly forgetful when it comes to recalling names of songs, movies and actors. In fact, so much so, that I can hardly tell you who played in the movie let alone the name of it, but I can draw motivating inspiration that spurs me to action from how it affected me. Please forget my name; it's not important! My desire is that something within these pages will affect your life for the better and in turn, inspire you to know that you too have influence to make this world a better place.

That may begin at your own dinner table, your own workplace, your own place of worship; all the encounters that your day consists of can be affected by the simple inner reminder to extend some form of love to all that you meet and to keep an open eye for opportunities to be of service to fellow travellers. As I said, let my name and face dissolve into mist but let that mist energise you as you reach into the shadows and embrace the unembraceable.

CHAPTER ONE

People often talk about childhood memories, the importance of the early formative years, and the effects they have on our psyche; well I remember being born. It was a traumatic event; unfolding in a cold, stark, harshly lit, unwelcoming room, to meet an equally unwelcoming, ice-cold mother. I remember being rejected, and the nurses attempting to compensate for the lack of love by fussing over me and even being prompted to name me. I was Michelle to the ice-queen and Janette to the compassionate nurses. I was a thoroughly unwanted bastard child, though the nurses thought me beautiful and content.

The year was 1961 and my 21-year-old mother had her career to think about. Susanna was a pretty, petite, blonde, blue-eyed girl with intelligence and ambition. I was the result of her brief fling with Rod, a sexy, green-eyed Queenslander who was to shoot himself dead, on a beach, just over 20 years later.

My mother was certainly ahead of her time. She went on to manage huge construction teams, of maybe 800 men or more, building hospitals in places like the Congo. When

I try to picture her I always imagine her in steel-capped shoes and wearing a hard hat. I have never met her. At 16, I attempted, in vain, to uncover who had given birth to me. Eventually, at the age of 38, I tracked her down via a search agency and wrote to her. She had recently returned to Australia after 30 years. After my second letter to her she decided that was enough. She graciously supplied me with a brief medical background, a few scant details of my coming into existence, followed by an admonishing farewell that I was master of my own destiny and that now I should go forth and enjoy. The pregnancy, the signing over to the State of her newborn baby, and my many enquiries years later numbed her. She may have been my mother and my daughter's grandmother, but she just wasn't interested. She rejected me a second time.

But this time I could feel disappointment and anger towards her. She led me on. Her first letter to me appeared to be so open and full of understanding. She wrote that I could ask her any question I wanted to, which was what I wanted to hear. I'm not very good with superficial relationships; I thrive on forming intimate bonds with the people I meet. I love people to confide in me and my friends must be amenable to a good heart-to-heart discussion. Otherwise, what's the point of friendship? So she offered me this dream potential no-holds-barred opportunity and I could hardly believe it. She decided that we were going to undergo the process together, as calmly as possible without bludgeoning one another with guilt or sentiment. I was absolute in my agreement; I am one of those chameleon types, I reflect back to people what they need me to be. I used to think it was a sign of my weakness but then a friend told me that she envied my flexibility in

4

company. You can bring me anywhere and introduce me to anyone and I will be positively sociable.

I had always fixated on my mother; the fact that I also had an unknown father never really struck me. All I know about Rod was that he had blonde curly hair; I don't even know his surname. He never knew about me so God only knows what would have been his reaction had he not killed himself.

It is a daunting task to approach a birth parent who has given you up. They didn't want you the first time, so how are they going to be now that you are fully grown? I suppressed any expectations that she was lighting a candle for me on my birthdays or that she was a total nut-case, or an alcoholic, or that she would hate me with a vengeance. As it transpired, my mother was merely an unfeeling, cold businesswoman. Her having to carry me around in her belly for nine months and then spew me out into the world was, to her, simply unfortunate—nothing more and nothing less. She could have been kinder, or even just plain old polite, but she chose to be neither. The letter was cold and stark, like that birthing hospital room—thanks but no thanks. I wept at her betrayal; she completely wrong-footed me. Then I felt overwhelmed by a sense of release. No more wondering or fantasising about my real mother, no more time wasted on daydreams about our impossibly fantastic relationship. She didn't want me so now, after all this time, I didn't want her. Jackpot! I was free.

It wasn't all bad. As I said, she provided me with some medical background. She confirmed that I wasn't anorexic. My friends had been nagging me for years to put on weight, making me eat every last bite from my plate and watching to see whether I was making myself vomit after meals. When I denied I had an eating disorder, they would sagely nod their heads and tell me I was in denial! My birth-mother informed me that all her family get thin as they age. It was genetics. Now instead of worrying about me my friends envied me.

***

Looking back now, I can see how my younger life helped to form the person I am today. Don't ask me how, but I always knew I was adopted. As was my kid sister, Annabel. She is two and a half years younger than me. I remember my parents, Doug and Judy, going through the adoption process to get her and I remember the day they brought her home. It was normal to me and I just knew that I had arrived at this house the same way. They told me that I was the 'ideal' infant. I happily gurgled the days away in a secure family atmosphere. I was a typical Gerber's baby, straight off a baby food commercial, with a big toothy smile and a placid nature. My poor parents had no inkling of what they were letting themselves in for. They were all you could ask for in a parent; loving and nurturing. It made me feel special to think that they had chosen me.

My mother and father were very down to earth, with a quiet intelligence and dry sense of humour. My father had a big important job that he never made a fuss of, while my mother kept the house and also worked part-time. They had known each other for a good while before falling in love, and remained in contact with the friends that they hung out with before they married. There was a large group of them with plenty of 'in-marriages'. The group provided an excellent support network for all 'members' with a good social life.

My parents also joined a Diner's Club and ate out in a fancy restaurant once a month. They also enjoyed their culture and would regularly attend the ballet and theatre, as well as the cinema. In fact I probably owe my life-long love of the movies to them, and perhaps they also inspired me to see other places when I got older, as they loved to travel. To me that's a sign of a good marriage; they are still each other's best friend and enjoy going out together.

As I grew to kindergarten age my health became a concern to my parents. An extraordinary amount of time was spent sitting in doctor's offices with my anxious mother. I wallowed in the attention, which started me on a dangerous mindset that it pays to be sick. It took some work on my part but I perfected the role of patient and missed many a school day thanks to faked fevers, pseudo-appendicitis and illnesses without name or history. I was also opportunistic; when my sister contracted chicken pox I grabbed her spotty face and rubbed it up against mine, willing the germs to make a leap of faith. Alongside honing my 'acting sick skills' I became adept at dealing with the consequences, that is, the taking or not-taking of the medicine. I would pretend to swallow and then once my mother turned her back I silently spat into whatever was closest, the sink or the potted plants. Fortunately there were lots of potted plants in our house; they were probably the healthiest plants in Melbourne.

***

I hated school. It bored me and I failed to see the point of it. Amazingly enough, my report cards were reasonable as far as the grades went, though there was always the note about how bright I was and how wonderful it would be if

I only applied myself a bit more. English was my favourite subject and I also enjoyed art, but that was about it. I just wanted to have fun, from making my class-mates laugh to staring out the window, my head filled with video-dreams showing me killing dragons or joining the Merchant Navy. As I got older I would be accompanied on these adventures by a handsome beau, though I remained the hero. When I was five my grandmother told me about the courageous Joan of Arc responding to the angel's voice, so I knew that women were every bit as brave as men. I believed that one day I would be called by the angels to undertake a special and difficult mission. In the meantime I kept myself busy.

My grandmother was a great influence on me; she was a grand ol' dame. Her husband was made mayor of an infamous red light/drug addict district, St Kilda's, in Melbourne. Junkies were always to be seen hanging around, waiting for their next score. I was the flower girl at the 'Mayoral Inauguration', which required me to spend a ridiculous amount of the time at the hairdressers.

I had to be taught how to walk properly and how to present the flowers. It was a lot of pomp and ceremony that didn't really appeal to me. I wore a silk golden dress and had my hair done up in a beehive. My grandparents looked like royalty. Grandpop wore a long dark coat with a fur lined collar and over this was the massive gold Mayor's chain. My grandmother, or Mardy as we called her, wore a long golden silk dress with short sleeves. She also wore white gloves that went up to her elbows, and a matching purse. Her hair was like mine, in a beehive style and she had on her 'cat's eye' glasses with lots of old expensive jewellery. She was the more sociable of the two—my grandfather could look very serious and was quite reserved in his manner. She did lots of good work throughout her life, and actually received an MBE (Member of the British Empire) title in recognition of her contribution to charitable works. She came from a very pro-Royal family; her great-great-great grandmother worked for Queen Victoria. My grandmother was a very traditional woman with firm values but she also knew how to enjoy herself. She loved her brandy and regular days out at the horse races. She was also very spiritual and made sure that Annabel and I attended Sunday school and church; she would often quiz us on what we had learnt.

She knew lots of different types of people, including 'media-types', and was responsible for my 15 minutes of fame. She took me to a recording of the *Tarax Show*, a popular Australian TV show for kids. I was fascinated with the huge noisy studio audience and the colourful set. One of the show's highlights was when the camera panned the audience to find the child with the happiest smile.

I had practised my smile all morning and was impatient for action. The camera began to move along the rail above our heads and I almost pulled a muscle as I crunched up my face, widened my eyes and stretched my mouth as high as it would go. My grandmother gazed at me fondly as the camera stopped in front of me and the popular presenter, Happy Hammond, summoned me to the stage. I couldn't believe it and had to be gently pushed to my feet. I was led down and placed on Happy's lap—something which could never happen now—where I shakily answered some questions about myself. I won a prize for my Herculean efforts and cherished the experience for a long, long time after. Years later I discovered that my win had been 'fixed' by my doting grandmother. I guess it's not what you know but who you know in show business!

Melbourne was a great place to come from, and it will always be special to me despite the fact that I don't see it too often now. I thought it a beautiful place with all its greenery and fine beaches where I spent my summer holidays. There was a terrific mixture of people—very cosmopolitan indeed. I grew up in Brighton, a very respectable and well-to-do area, but I loved to explore the not so respectable places, of which there appeared plenty, or so it seemed to me, that were far more interesting.

There was a strong Anglo-Saxon and Celtic presence with the English, Irish, Scottish and Welsh communities, alongside plenty of Greeks, Italians, and later on, Japanese and Vietnamese. There were also a lot of World War II survivors who always seemed to stick out a bit. I fancied that they looked sadder than everyone else. Even their kids looked fretful; on hot summer days the tattoos from the concentration camps were unintentionally on show—a permanent reminder of horrible days gone by.

It's a strange thing—to think back to your childhood and search for silly details. It's a whole different world and you can hardly relate to the child you were. I remember I wanted to marry Elvis ... or Batman ... or Robin Hood. Innocence is such a fragile quality and once it's gone it's like having a child—you can barely remember life before everything changed forever.

My weekends as a kid strike me today as blissful even when I had my household chores; the car and house were usually scrubbed alike at the end of the week. My sister and I also helped with the gardening, tending the vegetables growing in the back yard.

During the summer months all housework would be followed by a romp in our swimming pool; pools were the normal prop in our well-off neighbourhood. Family outings were frequently organised, sometimes comprising of a picnic at the beach and sometimes a stay over in our caravan on the outskirts of Melbourne. I think this routine instilled in me a good work-ethic and the importance of sharing time with loved ones.

At the age of 11 it struck me that I disliked the size of my front teeth. Like most girls my age I was terribly insecure and self-absorbed about my looks and I spent many an hour staring at my teeth in the mirror, trying to find a solution to their hugeness. Then it hit me, and I marvelled at how long it took me to come up with the obvious and simple answer.

Armed with nothing more than nail clippers, I trimmed one of my teeth. Yep, that's right; I clamped the clippers on the tooth and pressed down until I heard the crunch. I cannot describe the pain; you will have to imagine it. Let me just say that the toughest inmates in Bang Kwang describe toothache as being the worst ache of all.

My immediate concern was that the tooth was now a great deal shorter than its neighbour. In pain but marvellously determined, I prepared to 'clip' the other tooth. Looking back now I don't know where I got my strength or guts— maybe I was thinking that if Joan of Arc could let herself be burnt alive then I could do this one little thing. Somehow I managed to cut the nerve and almost collapsed in pure—and I don't use these words lightly—unadulterated agony.

A few harrowing days passed before I dared to 'confess' that I had smashed my teeth on the drinking taps at school. Immediate dental attention was required. In fact, it took several years of dental work to repair the damage. I would like to be able to write that this was the only time I ever harmed myself, but I would be lying.

***

Up to the time when I approached my teens, I was, I suppose, a normal and obedient child, and though I tended not to pay as much attention as I might have in school, there were still some figures who influenced me in later life. One teacher, Mrs Cornish, did make an impact on me. I was 12 and in sixth grade when discussions of current affairs got my attention. She was a kind, intelligent lady with wrinkles and grey hair. She had a good bond with the class; if we didn't want to pursue a particular topic it was beyond easy to distract her to a subject that interested us more. She talked to us more than any other teacher. One day she told us that she had had hepatitis and therefore couldn't donate blood. We tut-tutted in sympathy and were appreciative of her sharing that with us. She was also the one that spoke to us about the Vietnam War; shocking us with its senselessness and shocking waste of life.

Looking at myself now, I am as far from the rebellious teenager I started out as, but at 13 I suddenly became a terrible-teen in public school. A lot of the boys were afraid of me and my best mate Carol. We would walk down the corridors jamming pins into kids' butts. I even carried a knife. One of our favourite pastimes was to ambush an unsuspecting guy; she would pull his pants down while I poured nail polish, or sand, into his pubic hair. Then, inevitably, we were busted. On one of our pin-jamming jaunts the school psychiatrist caught Carol in the act. I put my acting skills to good use again. During her scolding of Carol the shrink turned and said something to me. I went into 'angst- teen mode' and told her to fuck off. Before she could recover herself I theatrically threw my hands in the air and wailed something along the lines of 'you guys just never understand me' and woefully stomped off as if I was burdened with the problems of the world. She was hooked by my performance and gave chase. A few strides down the corridor she 'managed' to pull me into her office where she sat me down. She sat across from me, folded her arms on her desk, stared into my eyes and asked me, in a reverential tone, what was 'going on'. I couldn't really have given an answer. I just turned unruly.

God love her, but she lacked imagination, humour, colour and sense. She meant well but I despised her for what I perceived as her blatant stupidity. I did blind Homer proud in the tale I spun of a miserable and misguided youth. She spoke to me slowly as if I was three—text book psychology. When I swore it seemed to excite her, to heighten my trauma as it were. I told her about feeling alone in the world—I'm sure I must have mentioned being adopted and maybe threw in a long dirge about being rejected at birth. When our first talk finished she gave me a bunch of yellow cards that I was to fill in every day, like a journal, about how I felt and what was going on with me. I was also to report to her everyday because I was an 'at risk' case. I only went twice and there was nothing she could do about it because I intimidated her. I wanted her to get tough with me and draw a line in the sand but she didn't. By this stage my parents were trying to get me to meet with a counsellor. The family doctor had recommended a guy he knew. However, they were also too gentle with me and I replied with my then usual daintiness, 'Screw you! I'm not going to see some quack.'

My parents' ideal infant had long gone and in its place was a most unappealing, unruly, unsociable, untrained teenager. My bedroom became my refuge within the house. Posters of my idols were pasted wall to wall—AC/DC, Janis Joplin, Led Zeppelin, Suzi Quatro, David Bowie and the wonderful T-Rex. Sometimes I would sleep on the floor just to get a different perspective of the décor. My favourite possession was a big old radio that had to be plugged in. It lit up when you switched it on, and was a soothing presence in the dark of the night. Music was my religion now and the radio guided me off to sleep every night. Any bedtime reading that I indulged in was usually the latest copy of my parents' *Playboy*, which they 'hid' in the same place for years. I loved the interviews—of course!

***

We moved several times throughout my childhood, and always into better and bigger houses. Strangely though, my favourite room in any of our houses remained my father's 'study', the room where he pored over his law books. It was also the guest room with a very comfortable couch that could be converted into a bed. There was also a TV, and so it became the room where I would usher in my friends to watch a movie in privacy.

My parents weren't terribly strict but did place a lot of stock on routine. No matter what was going on in my life the routine seldom changed. Dinner was ready at the same time each evening and there was no TV during meals. We got up at the exact same time for years, to leave for our destinations at the exact same times. My room had to be kept reasonably tidy, and I washed the dinner dishes every night. Bedtime, until my teens, was between 8.30pm and 9pm, and then it was extended to 11pm. But then all hell broke loose as I started to 'explore' myself and my circumstances.

I think I was born old. I always asked questions and challenged any authorities that I came up against. Between the ages of seven and nine I had consistently questioned the Vietnam War, while in Sunday school I questioned the Bible and its teachings. No one ever gave me satisfactory answers on any account. From an early age my politics clashed with my father's. He believed that the dropping of the bombs on Hiroshima and Nagasaki was justified because it ended World War II, whereas I strongly disagreed. Bit by bit I found myself looking at the life of my parents. We always lived in a nice house, in a nice neighbourhood. The bills were always paid on time and my parents were never less than good people. But I found it all a bit wanting. I would think fervently that there must be more to life than this. I never liked Christmas or birthdays, which I found out later was to do with being adopted.

My birthday reminded me on a yearly basis that my mother had rejected me, while Christmas was all about the family, but not the one that I had been born into. I would feel lonely and empty on these occasions instead of joyous, which is what I assumed normal people felt. I always felt there was something missing but I could never figure out what that was. Fortunately, I appreciate my parents more now than I did then.

I felt different from the family. Annabel was the perfect daughter; meek and mild, until I moved out and then she suddenly became more assertive, as if my absence gave her room to grow. If she had any misgivings about being adopted she kept them to herself. She grew afraid of me because I was so horrible to her. The amount of times I forced her to eat wriggling snails!

Though we did join forces to try to force a distant friend of the family to eat dog poop and tried to poison the postman. I was seven and she was my four-year-old accomplice. Our grandmother had this fantastic place full of different things that we used to call our 'ransacking cupboard'. One day we found a can of Strepsils throat sweets, which looked like candy. We were just about to tuck in when our grandmother appeared and told us we couldn't eat them because they were medicine. She exaggerated her point by adding that they would make us sick because they were poisonous. We hastily put them back in their wrappers and I got the idea of poisoning our mailman. I was fascinated by the thought of watching someone die. So, Annabel and I spent ages trying to dissolve the Strepsils in water so it would look like red cordial. Finally, we succeeded and placed the glass, outside, on the top of the post box. We hid in the garden in the nick of time. The mailman arrived as we were still giggling hysterically. No doubt he heard us and knew what we were up to. Who in their right mind would pick up and drink from a strange glass anyway? He took out the post and ignored the glass. We rushed forward, 'Excuse me, Mr Postman, here's a glass of lemonade for you.'

He smiled an I-know-what-you-kids-are-up-to smile and said, 'Thank you very much,' and then rode off on his bicycle. We were so disappointed.

Annabel was the one who encouraged me to seek out my birth mother. She had gone through a difficult experience with her birth-parents. Her mother and father had given her up for adoption and had then married each other the following year. They were married for ten years before having a family, a boy and a girl, her 100% siblings. When Annabel tracked them down her parents didn't want to know her; they didn't want her coming to the house because how would they explain her to her innocent brother and sister? I always wonder if contacted parents think the surprise-out-of-the-blue is after their inheritance, plus the legitimate children usually don't like a possible usurper in their parents' affections. It took a while before they allowed her into their lives and answered her questions. I don't think that the relationship is a particularly warm one, even today.

***

Adopted children often react in one of two ways; shutting down or rebelling. They fear that they are going to be rejected a second time, by their adoptive parents. I really wish that someone could have explained this to my parents; I guess Dr Spock didn't include adoptive children in his book. I rebelled. I took my anger out on my parents, teachers and relatives—basically any authority I came up against. Looking back, I was a long way away from the person I am now, but perhaps it was necessary for me to live through these years and experience what I did, in order to develop.

On the plus side my social standing among my school-mates improved. I became a big party girl. Friends counted on me for a good time, or simply to stir up trouble. I began to drink copious amounts of alcohol and would fearlessly digest anything that resembled a drug.

It was the early 1970s in Melbourne when I hit my teens—a wild time indeed. Drugs were everywhere and underscored a life of freedom, in love and war. There was a secret hole under my bed where I kept my dope pipes and cigarettes. I hardly ever had to pay for drugs; I just went to parties and took whatever was on offer. As soon as I arrived a joint would be passed to me. People wanted me drunk and stoned because then I would lead the way with my antics, from dancing on the furniture to parading around nude. I would have everyone stripped within minutes and dancing as if nobody was watching. I was a hippie through and through. We all craved to be free of guilt, of hang-ups, of responsibilities. It was also the era of free love.

I lost my virginity some time before my 14th birthday. I was having a sleep over in my friend's house. We were in a youth church group and were being brought to see some movie—I think it was *Rollerball*. Why a church group would want to bring youngsters to that movie is beyond me. Anyway, I was doubly bored because I had already seen the movie so my friend Liz and I soon found ourselves chatting to the two cute guys sitting in front of us. After a bit we decided to sneak out of the cinema so that we could talk properly. The four of us headed to the park and had a joint between us. It was getting late so Liz said we had to go home and go to bed, as far as her parents were concerned. We duly went home, reported on the movie and then yawned that it was way past our bedtime. We bade her parents goodnight and headed for her bedroom.

Once we judged it safe we sneaked back out her bedroom window and met up with the two boys. One of them, Michael, had a free house as his parents were away, so we went there. At the house we divided into couples and went our separate ways. Michael took me around the house for a tour and we ended up having sex in his sister's bed—why I don't know. I even stole some money that she had left lying around, which was awful of me! We spent the night there and then Liz and I had to leave for her house early the next morning. The birds were already singing as we made our way back giggling and sharing details of our recent exploits. Unfortunately we made a lot of noise trying to get back into her house via the bathroom window and had her terrified parents thinking they were being burgled. Liz was a good friend and convinced her parents not to tell mine as they were very strict and would kill me if they heard about this. Of course this wasn't entirely true but it still spared me some hassle and grief.

My friends and I experimented with casual sex, with each other and with boys. Our parties began to encompass loving orgies. We would get stoned, strip and then start loving the ones we were with. We didn't meet to have an orgy, it simply happened, especially in the summer months when party revellers would be clad in bikinis and swim suits. I wasn't a slut—well, I suppose everyone says that—but I didn't sleep with truck loads of strangers. I believed in the hippie ethos that sex is a normal, natural, healthy way of connecting with someone. I was very sexually progressive and completely open about it. After all, what was so dreadfully wrong about being naked and fucking a beautiful friend, male or female? It was great fun; Pink Floyd on in the background, the smell of grass from room to room, and everyone happy and humping. There was no contraception or condoms around then and it's a miracle that there wasn't lots of us pregnant, but we never ever considered the consequences or, if we did, the thought of making babies didn't stop us from making love. We just lived for the moment.

After school we used to hang out at a local park. Everyone did. It was a big enough park with a busy pond inhabited by ducks and other birds. People from different schools would meet up there in the evenings to drink and get stoned. Older guys would turn up on their motorbikes or in their stolen cars. I was fascinated by these guys. They exuded this coolness and almost incidentally instilled fear in us younger ones. My background was so far removed from worn leather jackets, stolen methods of transport and the air of potential danger. Some were drug addicts and some were ex-cons and I loved being in their company. To this day I feel completely comfortable around addicts and criminals—their conversation is very refreshing to me.

However fraught things got, I didn't care. Nights spent sleeping on the beach could erupt into warfare between skinheads and biker gangs. I didn't discriminate between them, as everyone was my friend. The guys, even the meanest looking ones, would open up to me with their worries, whether it was about a girl they liked or some rough experience in their home life.

My big mouth used to get me into trouble though. One night I was sitting beside the brother of a friend of mine. He was part of a biker crowd and boasted that his bedroom was painted black with drips of red paint to represent blood. I thought he was great. His nickname was Weasel and he was a nasty, mean individual, but I had a crush on him. I was maybe 13 or 14 at the time. I started to row with him over something or other and suddenly he was trying to choke me. He was pissed and I probably was too. He had me pressed up against the wall and might have killed me had not his friend pulled him off me. They ended up having a punch-up which their friendship never fully recovered from. People blamed me for it afterwards because it was said that I had come between them.

When I think of the risks I took, I shudder. My friends and I would hitchhike in our full hippie regalia; men would pick us up in their cars, offer us a joint and invite us out to get stoned at their place. I honestly can't say how many times I woke up in some apartment or house not knowing the owner or remembering how I got there. Nevertheless, I did have some sort of survival instinct which kicked in when necessary. One time a friend and I found ourselves in the house of a much older guy and his friends. They plied us with drinks; I willingly gulped down a pint glass of straight whisky. Then a large joint was passed around. Despite my being stoned I sensed that the atmosphere was becoming sinister. My friend was almost legless and it suddenly struck me that we were probably going to be gangbanged if I didn't act fast. My guardian angel must have helped me drag my friend to her feet and out the door. Fortunately the men were as drunk and stoned as we were. I saw a tram stop to let some passengers off and half-dragged-half-carried my friend towards it. The men were behind us, whooping and hollering vulgar threats. I knew they wouldn't try anything on public transport. Miraculously we made it on to the tram. My friend collapsed face down on the floor as it slowly moved off and I was too stoned to help her, but we were safe. The people on the tram gasped in shock at the state of us—our eyes must have been in the back of our heads, I could hardly focus and she looked dead to the world. Obviously we were a cause for some concern because the tram stopped in front of a police station and I thought, 'Shit, we're dead'. People were gesturing to the approaching officers as I, once again, found the strength to lift my friend for another chase, this time with the police. I carried her for as long as I could and then spotted a garage that had been left open. Without thinking I dropped her to the ground and pushed her under the car and followed her. There we lay, silently, in pools of oil and grime as we heard the officers call out to one another, looking for us. I thought they were never going to give up. We waited for what seemed like an eternity before feeling brave enough to come out of our hiding place and trudge home.

***

Before too long I had acquired my first serious boyfriend, Simon. I was the envy of many a girl. Simon was a bit of an icon whose tough, rough reputation was known throughout the land. One tale that was spread around was about how he had broken his mother's arm during a row. He had a fierce temper and was quite confrontational. He wasn't tall but made up for his lack of height with a swarthy muscular build and Italian good looks; he looked and acted a lot older than his 16 years, with his full beard and many tattoos. We met in the park one night when he 'rescued' me from under a big lump of a guy who was trying to hump me while we were both off our heads after a joint. I was never really taken in by his reputation—tough guys aren't always so tough. As an Italian Aussie, Simon had to deal with a lot of crap from 'pure white' Aussies. The Greeks and Italians were called 'wogs' and life on the street could be somewhat precarious, especially if you were a signed up member of a biker-cum-Sharpie gang.

We got along quite well and shared some mad times, thanks to the amount of grass we smoked. He stole a car once when he was completely off his head, resulting in him hitting some poor pedestrian because he was too stoned to steer. Fortunately the pedestrian lived. I regularly came off his motorbike when he was attempting to drive when wrecked but of course I never really hurt myself because I would be equally bombed. Our early dates were quite conservative; we'd eat out at a Chinese restaurant and then go see a movie. Our madder dates would see us skulling bottles of vodka or Bacardi; you would hold the bottle upside down and keep gulping the drink down the back of your throat until the bottle was empty. I was the fastest 'skuller' around and was quite proud of myself. These big biker dudes would watch me drink in admiration and give me a round of applause. The silliness started when a paralytic Simon and me would get on his motorbike or behind the wheel of a car and drive up the edge of the cliffs near the beach, as close to the edge as possible, for the sheer madness of it.

As a nod to the times we had an open relationship. We were both free to indulge our desires with others—well, except, as it turned out, for me. One of my girlfriends, Sandy, was anxious to lose her virginity, preferably with someone she knew. I always prided myself on being a good friend; I asked her if she liked Simon and she said yes. So I asked my boyfriend to do me a favour and sleep with her. I thought it was a very nice gesture on my part. Both parties agreed and shortly afterwards she was no longer a virgin and I even got to watch from the next room while quietly toking on a joint, and listening to 'Another Brick in the Wall'. She thanked me profusely and I thanked Simon for helping me out and all was right with the world; that is until I wished to indulge myself at a party with an attractive boy called Johnny.

I dragged Johnny to the master bedroom to act out a few stoned fantasies. Then I duly informed Simon who, to my horror, went utterly berserk. I had never seen what jealousy could do to a person. We were in my friend's house, celebrating her 14th birthday. I remember there was this fabulous chandelier on the ground that had yet to be hung up. Simon, screaming like a wounded animal, lifted the precious piece and kicked it across the room where it shattered into pieces against the wall. He was like a different person, a mad man. He was chasing the party-goers and trying to lash out at them with his fists and feet. He kept punching the walls and kicking the doors. Everyone fled, either out of the house or upstairs. I cowered in the bathroom, listening to him yelling my name and shouting, 'Come here you fucking bitch. I'm gonna kill you, I'm gonna kill you all.'

After a few minutes of this I decided that enough was enough. The fact that everyone was hiding from him was making him worse. He seemed to be relishing in the idea that he was scaring people; it was empowering his performance-tantrum. 'Screw this!' I thought; as I went out to confront him. I met him in the dining room and spoke as calmly as I could.

'Simon stop this. You are just trying to scare the shit out of us. Stop showing off, I'm not afraid of you.'

While I was not exactly expecting him to hang his head in shame and say sorry in a contrite voice, I didn't expect what actually happened. I felt like a part of me had stepped aside to watch the unfolding events, because in no way did I think that when he drew back his fist it was to punch me savagely in the face. My nose seemed to fly across my cheek as I watched him pull his fist back again. I don't know if he meant to hit me again, but he stopped when he saw how much blood was spewing from my face after that first punch. My face blew up and changed colour. The others crawled out of their hiding places to stare in fascination at my almost unrecognisable features. As usual we were all drunk and stoned, so there was a lot of, 'Wow man, your face is awesome,' comments, as opposed to someone rushing me to the nearest ER. The birthday girl later became a prostitute and later again, went off the rails completely. The two of us were from the same kind of background; upper middle class in a good neighbourhood—it was a time of rebellion for all of us I think.

Would you believe that Simon and I went on to have a deep meaningful discussion that evening after things quietened down? He was very upset by what he had done to me and was a little in shock. We talked about life and where we were going. We both admitted to feeling lost in general. I don't remember the conversation in great detail but I do know that I counselled him for hours, trying to help him find some direction in his life. It was the start of a life-time of having men confide their innermost thoughts and fears to me. We also needed to concoct a credible story for my parents. I wasn't very imaginative and told them that my purple and blue face was the result of me running full-speed into a door post.

My own 14th birthday was a few days later, and I spent it with masking tape over my nose, barely able to see out of my swollen eyes. To celebrate, two of my closest friends and I went to the cinema to see *Frankenstein's Bride*—I think I received more gasps of horror than the film did. Once again I enjoyed shocking people with my looks. Several hospital visits followed and I had to have my face re-set. Later on I needed Simon's help. Because Johnny and Simon were no longer talking, their mutual friends were out to get me since, once again, it was all my fault. They were hoodlums who had nothing better to do with their time. One of his friends informed Simon that he would kill me for my insult to him. There was nothing that Simon could say to placate the situation, so he did the next best thing. He got me a revolver and some bullets. He loaded the gun for me and I didn't dwell on the fact that I hadn't the slightest idea how to use it. I carried it around in my Indian hippie bag; I was a loved up hippie with a 'piece', instead of peace! After a few days I returned it to him. I decided that I would prefer to be killed than kill someone. I didn't take the threat lightly and only realised how scared I was when the next door neighbour woke me up late one night. I slept at the back of our house and he drove his motorbike down his driveway past my window. I jumped up screaming, thinking I was going to die.

The threats disappeared over time. Six months later Karma hit Simon hard when he had his own face and nose broken by a gang of skinheads armed with pool cues. Witnesses said he was whimpering under a pool table as they beat him repeatedly. A few years later I attended the funeral of the guy who had wanted to kill me. He had died in a freak car accident.

***

When the hippie fashion started to fade we all became 'Sharpies'. There were different groups of Sharpies, depending on where you came from or who you hung out with. I shaved my hair to a buzz cut but left a long tail of blonde hair falling from the skinhead. We looked like Natalie Portman in V For Vendetta and got a lot of stares in the street, which I revelled in. The costume was mostly jeans, cool cardigans (yes, there are such a thing!) and big boots with a chisel toe and a Cuban heel; we wanted to look like bikers. We also wore very militant-style jackets and probably more successfully resembled Hitler's Youth! I recently found a web site devoted to Sharpies—I never realised that I was part of Melbourne's folklore; Sharpies were unique to Melbourne because it had nothing to do with outside influences. We weren't—for once—following either an American or English style, and our music was restricted to Melbourne bands.

I sort of drifted in and out of being a biker, Sharpie and hippie for some time but gradually peace, love and tie-dye clothes won out.

I much preferred being a hippie and felt it suited me better. The hippie culture just appealed more to me and suited my personality. I was a real flower child; I wanted to be free and shed all the weight of expectation and responsibility that society places on you. I stopped wearing a bra because how could you be free if your breasts were rigid? … or something like that. My bags were beaded affairs covered in little mirrors; I wore a beret with John Lennon-type glasses, the little round ones. I only wore silver jewellery and lots of it. I even made some of my own jewellery; being a hippie brought out my artistic and creative streak.

Nevertheless, however I styled my hair, I continued to drink and do drugs like there was no tomorrow. There wasn't any ecstasy or cocaine in Australia at the time. I mostly stuck with grass, LSD, and prescription pills. I popped uppers and downers as if they were sweets. Fortunately I didn't particularly like heroin when I tried it—God knows I would not be here if I had. I smoked Buddha Sticks; marijuana laced with opium. Although, even if I had liked it there wasn't too much of it about and I wasn't going to start spending a fortune I didn't have. What I did have was something of a death wish; I imagined myself dead and beautiful with a needle stuck into my arm—somehow I envisaged this as a suitably dramatic way to go. Tragedy had a huge appeal for me and I really wasn't too interested in a tomorrow. I was drinking lunatic amounts of hard liquor. You might have difficulty believing that I would regularly down an entire bottle of Bacardi and not stop gulping until every last drop was gone. But I did. I drank not just to get drunk, but to get absolutely paralytic. I had absolutely no regard for my personal safety. I wouldn't know where I was or who I was with. Sometimes I would wake up to discover that I had been beaten up, and possibly worse, but would have no memory of the previous evening. I had been stealing alcohol since I was 12. I devised 'Jungle Juice', which was basically a pint of as many different drinks as you could pilfer. Naturally it was extremely powerful stuff that would blow your head after one dose.

I had started smoking cigarettes at seven and by the time I was in my early teens I was smoking before school, during the lunch break and after school—cigarettes or grass, whatever was handier. Possibly it was as much for the social aspect as it was for the nicotine; smoking was rarely done alone. I also varied my drugs with sniffing—glue, petrol, aerosols or whatever I could get my hands on. Petrol, which was easy to obtain, was a particular favourite, so much so that friends called me 'Petrol Head'. I nearly accidentally set myself alight one day when I confused my head with the petrol can; instead of pouring the petrol back into the can I poured it over my head and then reached for a cigarette and lighter. Thankfully my stoned friends managed to wrestle the light from me. They rushed me to the house of this much older guy who we found ourselves turning to in matters of crisis. After rolling his eyes to Heaven at the sight of my head, he patiently and laboriously washed the petrol out of my hair.

He and his house mates were real playboys and there were always lots of women hanging around there but it was a place where we crashed without bother. I never knew for sure what they did for a living. For some reason they all struck me as the sort of blokes who sold nice cars. There was always good music on no matter what time of the day or night we turned up at. They had a great record collection and the best stereo around, not to mention their bar. Money obviously wasn't a problem. They seemed to spend an inordinate amount of time playing billiards and pool, and what made this even more interesting for the casual observer was that they played naked. They were young handsome bachelors who knew exactly how to enjoy themselves. They knew we were underage so they didn't touch us.

It was also at their house that I 'fixed' a tattoo that I had given myself at a friend's house and then didn't like. I was determined to remove it. I had created a girl gang and we called ourselves 'Hound Digger'—don't ask me why. We carried knives and acted very tough; perhaps our attempt at feminism or women's lib. I was leader and went by the name of 'Skull', which referred to my envied drinking skills. Anyway I had thought that a dagger would look good but it didn't. So I soaked some cotton wool in bleach and placed it on the tattoo, then briefly set the cotton wool alight so that it would burn the top of the tattoo. It seemed like a good idea at the time! Then I let the bleach remain on my wounded arm and bandaged the whole thing up so that the bleach would continue to eat into the tattoo … and my skin. Needless to say there were problems. The bleach did its job very well but then my arm became infected. I went around to the guy's house and he freaked out when he saw my messy wound, saying, 'Oh sweet Jesus you're gonna get gangrene!' He made me go to his house every day so he could wash out my arm and bandage it correctly. By the time it healed I then had an ugly tattoo and a scar; however, as soon as I could I had a nicer tattoo of a rose drawn over the ugly one and it all worked out fine.

I was a functional addict, though maybe 'addict' is not the right word. I didn't have a drug of choice and I certainly wouldn't have held up a pharmacy in order to get drugs. I didn't crave drugs or alcohol. I just took them if they were there. It was more a case of, 'Let's live life to the max!' mixed up with self-destructive behaviour. I was breaking all the boundaries in the hope that someone would erect some especially for me. I would walk around naked, pick a fight with someone twice my size, shoplift, drive wrecked, stolen cars and take rides on ridiculously speeding motorbikes. I was always the entertainer and entranced an audience of friends with my one-woman shows, where I might slash myself with razor blades, burn both arms with cigarettes, pierce my body with large needles and a host of other bizarre party tricks. I would get a false sense of bravado from my friends' amazement and it would push me further for a bigger 'wow' factor.

I was functional in that I could get up everyday, stoned or drunk, and go to school. Nobody seemed to notice my glassy stoned stare in class; I knew how to lay low and behave myself. I have a real instinct for that. At this point you are probably wondering about my parents and whether they had any idea of what was going on. They did. One day I walked into my bedroom and knew instinctively that someone had been going through my things. My diary had been moved. I didn't react; I just sort of accepted it. If my mother had read it they now knew everything. I always felt that they didn't buy my smashing my nose against a doorpost. I waited for a row to erupt when my father came home from work but nothing happened. Everyone continued to treat me as normal. We ate our dinner and the plates were cleared away. I did my homework and went to bed. My parents had decided that a stormy confrontation wouldn't serve any purpose; they were very wise like that. Instead, a couple of days later, my mother was giving me a lift somewhere. Just as I was about to gruffly take my leave and get out of the car she quietly said, 'Susan, we know you're trying and doing things that you shouldn't be doing. But we also know how smart and intelligent you are. We trust you to know the difference between right and wrong.'

I mumbled something smart and intelligent like, 'Yeah, yeah,' but their strategy did leave an impression on me, and it's a technique that I have since used with my own teenage daughter today.

When they asked me what I wanted to do with my life I would act smart and brattish and tell them that I wanted to be a garbage collector. Then they would ask me again and I told them that I wanted to be an actress. As I've said my grandmother had a few connections with the theatre and media world and my parents thought about trying to get me into an acting school in St Kilda's. Nothing came of this however. I think they thought me a little young and preferred me to finish high school first. They were never heavy-handed or forbidding with me. They always kept the lines of communication open between us—none of this banishing me to my room without supper stuff. In truth

I was very stoned most of the time in the house and they never realised. I remember my poor father coming into my room one evening to talk to me about something. I don't remember now what he said because I didn't have a clue what he was talking about then, thanks to being completely off my face. He rested his hand on my TV, and just inches away from his fist was a massive joint, about six inches long and one inch thick, but he never saw it.

***

My cousins were attending a posh, co-ed, private school in Melbourne and my poor parents decided that this could be the making of me. I howled when I heard about it but they were adamant that I should, at least, try it. I was 14 years old; with my nose and face in a bloody cast which was inscribed with 'Fuck You'. Unsurprisingly, no one rushed to befriend me on that first awful day. The school was full of rich, snobby kids who all surfed and rode horses; well that's what it seemed like. To say I was a novelty is an understatement. There were rules, rules and more rules that only served to push my rebellious side creatively. I was told I couldn't pluck my eyebrows so I shaved mine off; I was told that I couldn't wear five earrings in my ears so I put in safety pins instead; I was told that I couldn't dye my hair so I shaved it all off too. Sometimes I would substitute the safety pins for tampons—imagine that, getting on the tram to school with tampons dangling from my ears. My outrageousness always seemed to involve public transport. I especially liked to spray my upper body with body paint and then put on a completely transparent top, just to see how uncomfortable it made passengers on the bus or tram.

My cheeks burn when I remember the party that my grandparents threw for their 50th wedding anniversary. I got chatting to this 'hip' pastor, who was maybe 40-ish and probably prided himself on being able to connect with young people. That sounds sarcastic and I don't mean to mock him because he seemed like a nice guy. It's just that he met me during my smartass period. I was wearing a colourful and mostly see-through hippie dress; what I wasn't wearing was a bra, and I kept daring him, silently, to look at my breasts. Finally he passed some remark about my dark tan and I, brazen as you like, pointed out that I didn't even have any white strap-marks. He smiled to himself as I pouted away in a manner I imagined to be provocative, but in hindsight probably made me look the young ignorant brat I was.

People tended to steer clear of me in school, out of fear as well as everything else. When the initial shock-factor wore off there were some muttering of distaste from the older girls. Apparently they didn't like my attitude and thought that I needed to be brought down a peg or three. A group of them let it be known that they were going to beat me up after school. Of all people it was Simon who once again saved the day for me. On the day of the arranged 'pegging down' he and his mate Patrick skidded up to the school fence, during recess, in a noisy pink and grey battered, stolen car. They fell out of it while swigging bottles of gin—no tonic—and started ogling the girls and calling out insults to the boys. Simon then yelled at the general school body to fetch Susan immediately. His demand was instantly met as 30 excited pupils came tearing through the school to tell me that my boyfriend was outside wanting to see me. I suppressed a smile and headed out to the two mean-looking hoods. Patrick just looked nasty and angry, while Simon had a chipped tooth, evil-looking beard, six-pack abs and an absolute foul-mouth. I felt like the Pied Piper of Hamelin as the 30 followed me back out to the fence to watch the re-union. Most of these kids had led very sheltered lives and would never have had any dealings with the likes of Simon. They stood gaping as I shot the breeze. Although Simon and I had broken up by this stage we were still good friends.

The visit worked wonders for my status in school. Now people sought me out because I was crazy and fun. A new circle of friends followed me around and I soon corrupted the lot of them. Once again I led the way in partying and encouraged them to drink and smoke grass, strip and lose their virginity. I even encouraged a few to come out of the closet. I'm sure I was the teachers' worse nightmare, heightened considerably by my newfound popularity. I suppose it was only a matter of time before I was suspended. I got into a fight with another girl, who was actually one of my best friends. We started ribbing one another, then pushing and shoving, then pulling hair and kicking in a frenzy. We managed to rip off each other's uniforms, down to our panties, and I wasn't wearing a bra. We were both sent home in a taxi to our parents, suspended for six days. I was in my gym uniform since the other one was in tatters. My parents had to pay the taxi fair and I thought it was all great fun.

After a year and a half of paying outlandish fees to the private school, my parents finally conceded defeat and I was back in public school. Strangely enough the private school never really gave me much trouble no matter what I did, until a few years later when I returned to the school to show them that I had grown into a relatively normal adult. The teachers were stunned to see the difference in me and I was acutely embarrassed when they recalled my youthful misdemeanours. I was living proof that miracles do happen. However, it was a bit of shock when the school later phoned my family and told them that I was welcome to visit any time but that they could not allow me to hand out Christian literature or talk about God to the pupils. And this was a Christian school!

CHAPTER TWO

I t was inevitable that things had to change for me. I was lost in my own little world, and I needed something to bring me back to reality and save me from myself.

I had had an epiphany. The year was 1977 and I was ready for a change. I spent the school summer break working part-time and had amassed quite a fortune. My friends and I decided to pool our resources and finish the break with a couple of weeks by the sea. We got drunk and stoned every day. I did a lot of LSD and was tripping the light fantastic and having incredible revelations. One night we went to see a movie showing Jimi Hendrix in concert and I started to think about the world we lived in: why was there war and hatred? What are we here for? The more I tried to drown out these questions in booze and drugs the louder they got in my head, and the more depressed I got.

I was looking for meaning and was reviewing my belief system. I believed that everyone had a reason for being, a destiny that they had to pursue. What was mine? I was desperate for direction, to find something that I could commit to. I was looking for a cause, and had even tried being a vegetarian but after seven days I had a burger, so that wasn't it. When I thought of another year in school, interspersed with drunken parties and my twisted social antics, it made me feel hollow. I was burnt out. And at such a young age. I cut short my beach holiday and headed home, where my depression deepened. I couldn't even drink or enjoy a joint.

I called over to a friend one Sunday and admitted my turmoil to her; 'I'm thinking of joining the Hari Krishnas or else I'm afraid I'm gonna kill myself!'

She hugged me and said, 'Look let's head out and get stoned, then if you still feel the same tomorrow you can join the Hari Krishnas next week.'

That seemed as good a plan as any. We walked out into the warm afternoon and hitchhiked over to the red light district where there was always something happening. Every Sunday there was a sort of market in St Kilda's, with a variety of buskers and music, and hippies selling their art and handcrafts; usually I bought as much stuff as I could carry and always left wanting more. This time I could barely muster the energy to look at the paintings. I surveyed my surroundings listlessly; there were crowds of people milling around, licking ice-cream cones and drinking beer, having a good time—but no one seemed to me to be really happy. The whole scene, my life; past, present and future, just seemed pointless. I looked across to the speeding traffic on the highway and sent up a silent appeal to whatever was listening: 'If you are real, you'd better do something quick because I can't go on like this. I'd rather die'.

Just then I heard music and people cheering and clapping. I crossed over to see what they were looking at. It was a play that had been put on by the roadside. I found myself forgetting about my problems and I watched the players.

One was a smiling hippie strumming a sitar and another was a beautiful woman doing ballet. The theatre group was an eclectic bunch of Christians, of all types and ages. They weren't about damnation and eternal guilt and sin, but were instead about hope and creativity and meaning—all of which I was starving for. Some of them were full-time Christian Aid workers and others just did it on their days off, all hoping that they might even just reach out to one person. Well, they certainly did that day, and that person was me.

I approached them afterwards. I was in my usual hippie attire; my long flowing Indian skirt, my tiny embroidered shirt that just stopped below my breasts, the back of my jacket was emblazoned with the wise words: 'Life is like a shit sandwich, the more dough you have the less shit you eat,' and bird bones and feathers hung from my ears. They looked me up and down and smiled. I looked like Mary Poppins on crack. I shyly greeted them and a conversation was quickly struck up. I warmed in particular to two of the guys. One was a gentle American whose name I'm ashamed to say I cannot remember. He had come from a very religious background but he wasn't, thankfully, religious himself. He did have this amazing knowledge of the Bible; he must have read it many times, but he wasn't egotistical about it.

I cannot abide self-righteous people, especially when their theme is staid religion. Another guy, John, who has remained a good friend of mine, asked me my name and where I came from, what I did and if I believed in Jesus. He was a regular hippie, like myself, with a certain wisdom and calmness that literally compelled me to tell him every mad thing I had done over the previous couple of years—including wanting to kill myself out of sheer weariness.

One of them said, 'If you're going to throw your life away, why don't you give it away instead?'

The hairs went up on the back of my neck and I shivered with the clarity of those words. It was like they truly recognised me and what I was going through. It all just seemed to make perfect sense. I could stop destroying my own life and start to help others with theirs. I wasn't sure if I could be as spiritual as them though, considering my outlook, and I told them that I went to church but it bored me because I could find nothing stimulating or challenging about the weekly rituals. To my surprise they nodded in agreement and pointed out that I could be a spiritual person without organised religion and tradition. I could invite Jesus into my life in a very intimate manner, which would be more challenging and much more personal than sitting in the back of a church on a Sunday morning. I prayed with them in the middle of that crowded street. I asked for help with changing my life; for the first time ever I felt inspired and it had nothing to do with a joint. I didn't see any bright lights, or hear a chorus of angels, but I felt profoundly moved. I could change my unsatisfactory life; I could do something and make a difference, a real positive difference. They introduced Jesus as this very real guy who wanted to take care of me and help me reach my potential. I was suddenly intoxicated by hope and love.

★★★

I stopped doing drugs from that day, and I managed it, miraculously, without needing rehab. I felt such peace in my heart that I knew my addictions were more about my emotional and mental state. Some time later I did try marijuana again, but it was horrible. It gave me such a major downer and made me paranoid—I knew that I would never touch it again. I preferred to work through my pain now instead of dosing myself with medication. I had more energy and was much livelier. I'm afraid that my friends didn't appreciate my transformation and I can't say that I blame them. I just felt so detached from my previous wild existence.

They missed the Susan who would liven up parties after skulling a bottle of hard alcohol and just didn't know what to do with this new version of me. There didn't seem to be any middle ground. I did continue to see them infrequently but my new outlook was like a glass barrier between us— we could see each other but just couldn't hear one another properly.

I informed my parents that I wanted out of school. I was 16 years old. I spent ages working on a speech in my head and had to wait until the two of them were together, and in a relaxed mood. I was prepared to fight a long drawn-out battle and to beg like a child, but it wasn't required. My parents weren't foolish; they could see that school wasn't stimulating me, or sending me on the path to a fulfilling career. They listened to my impassioned plea for liberation from academia, glanced quickly at one another, and by the next morning, gave me their blessings. That very afternoon they took me down to the principal's office and she gave me permission to leave school. There was some necessary paperwork to be filled out and I needed all my teachers to sign my release. Nearly every teacher was in class and I had to interrupt them. Invariably they asked me, in front of the students, why I wanted to leave and what I planned to do, and invariably I replied, 'I'm going to change the world!' I was probably one of the most well-known characters in the school thanks to my wild reputation, and I could see that my answer was impressive to these staid youngsters. I felt I walked out of school that day in a blaze of glory.

My parents were more than a little dubious about my sudden change. I think they expected it to last as long as my vegetarian phase did. They were pleasantly surprised when I didn't revert back to 'angry young teenager' mode after a couple of weeks and so were prepared to go along with my wanting to quit school.

I joined the Christian group and received a lot of much needed counselling and training so that I could help others. I will always be grateful to the group because they gave me direction and were pretty instrumental in helping me become who I am today. It was basic community stuff. We put on shows for kids, we visited prisoners in jail who had nobody else to talk to, and wrote letters to them. We would visit the homes of disabled people to see how we could help them and their families. We also held a Saturday night party for the local teenagers and would put on some entertainment for them. It was a rough part of town so they weren't exactly queuing up on the street outside but still we managed to attract a few token toughies.

When I felt I was ready I began to counsel people. It always amazes me; the amount of people who don't have life sussed and imagine that they are the only ones who are cocking up. There are so, so many of us who are terrified of making mistakes, feel lonely and isolated, and have been through some amount of shit in their lives. People seemed to trust me and wanted to tell me their worries, perhaps because I could show them my tattoos, scars, and many piercings. I could talk realistically about drugs and drink and nothing impressed me because I had already been there—I couldn't judge people since I had made the same or even worse mistakes. I didn't use big words because I didn't know them myself and I couldn't patronise anyone because I was still in my teens.

I had a new reason to get up in the morning and new friends to hang out with. I guess it was only a matter of time before a happier and healthier me attracted someone new into my life—there hadn't been anyone serious since Simon. I was 17 years old when I met Peter, a gentle fun-loving hippie, who was four years older than me. There is that famous line from Charlotte Bronte's novel *Jane Eyre* when she says, 'Reader I married him.' I would have to a make a slight change to that: 'Reader I could have married him,' because he did ask me! He was the first guy to ever propose to me but I didn't take him up on it, although, we did have an informal ceremony, where we exchanged vows of love, in front of friends and, even, my parents. This was their compromise for not allowing us to marry. He was lovely; a long-haired hippie who wrote his own music, travelled nowhere without his guitar, shared my love for Janis Joplin and Jimi Hendrix, and my love for helping others. I had been about to leave Melbourne for Queensland where I had accepted a job as nanny. The family had been recommended to me. I love kids and was ready to see more of Australia so it seemed perfect, until I found myself falling for Peter. He took me out for a hot chocolate on the day I was to catch my train and quietly asked me not to go. And so I stayed!

***

We actually set up home together in a mobile home for a while. It was a bit of a shock living with a man. I discovered that I was still quite selfish and needed to learn how to share my life with someone else. We lived and worked together for two years, travelling around Australia and finding people who needed our help. It was a lovely two years; just living day to day and meeting all sorts of people in all sorts of places. This really opened my eyes to the world outside of the limited life I had so far experienced. When money was tight we managed to get odd jobs, though Peter frequently made a bundle busking on the streets. His good looks and warm smile usually had people reaching into their pockets for some coins.

Pete's brother Brian was working in a uranium mine in the middle of nowhere, Jabiru, about 300km from the city of Darwin, the capital of the Northern Territory. Darwin was the scene of Australia's worst natural disaster to date when Cyclone Tracy hit on Christmas morning in 1974. At 3am the anemometer at Darwin Airport recorded winds of 217km an hour, just before it stopped working. In all, 65 people died that day, 16 were lost at sea and never found, and 1,000 people needed medical attention. Brian got Pete a job in the mine, so we headed down there.

It was a long, dusty, stifling drive into a very desolate area—small shrubbery bushes were the only things to be seen for miles around. Jabiru got its name from the large jabiru bird, so named by the Aboriginals. The bird was also known as the 'Police-bird' and 'Black-necked stork'. In 1970 uranium was discovered at Ranger in Arnhem Land, with more uranium discovered the following year at Jabiluka. Uranium is the principal ingredient for fuelling nuclear weapons and nuclear reactors—the raw material of the nuclear industry, the most lethal industrial process on earth. There were years of heated debate over whether or not to mine the uranium, but money won out in the end. There was good reason for anger and fear of the mine and the damage it could do to the environment. The Kakadu National Park was established in the area in 1979 and houses more than a third of Australia's bird population. It's also contains some of the country's best preserved archaeological sites, along with extensive rock art galleries. Aboriginal people have been living here for countless years so you can only imagine the importance of the area to them.

We had to be cleared by security before we could access the camp. That was a tough life, especially for the 15 women working alongside the thousand or so highly testosteroned, boorish, loud-mouthed men. Now, this might sound like Heaven on earth to some girls out there but I tell you honestly that the place was utterly devoid of romance and sentiment! Of course there were some sweet lonely guys who quickly became favourites with me, Pete, and Brian. The three of us got on very well and kept each other sane during the hot, hot evenings when the working day was over.

I worked with the handful of women in the kitchen. These women were tough; they had to be, and though I admired them I didn't envy them their life-style or want to ape their toughness. We didn't stay there past a couple of months and I was glad to leave. It was a strange isolated society that was built around manual labour. Life was regimental thanks to the rules of the camp. There was nothing cosy about the place—the men slept in cheap mobile homes that thankfully had air-conditioning. There was a drive-in cinema and plenty of bars but that was it as far as their social life went. I befriended one of the women, a mother of three young kids, and would accompany her when she went to the city to buy supplies once a month. You could buy stuff at the camp but it was generally marked up. The wages in the camp were really good—they had to be to attract people to work there in the first place. Anyway, getting back to civilisation once a month was worth the long drive. I couldn't wait to have a coffee in a nice café and stroll through shops that would normally not interest me in the least. I felt I had returned from living on a strange planet and actually got some pleasure from looking at the relatively busy high street in Darwin.

There was also a lot of wild life; well, more than I was used to in Melbourne. The nearby rivers ran into the ocean so you could frequently see sharks cavorting not too far from crocodiles. On one of our trips I saw the biggest snake I have ever seen in my life. It was a massive python and was slowly making its way across the quiet road. We drove over it and it was like going over a ramp. I was astonished to look back and see it continue on its way as we did ours, none the worse for having had a car loaded down with supplies on its back. That snake summed up life in the uranium mine camp; no matter what, you just did what you had to do, without fuss or ceremony.

My years with Pete taught me that I was a born traveller, and paved the way for much of my life, constantly on the go. I just felt so free with my one small suitcase and backpack. I had few clothes and possessions but felt rich in myself. There is an amazing hitch-hike / backpacking network to be availed of; we met and befriended so many like-minded travellers of all nationalities, it was a complete revelation to me. I loved Perth and Queensland. The people in these two places were exceptionally friendly and I especially loved the mix of building styles in Perth—modern and colonial. Then again

I loved the fabulously beautiful and cosmopolitan city that is Sydney, with its many beaches and parks. I'm a sucker for the beach!

Nevertheless, I think one of the most memorable places was, for me, the cliffs of Nullaboor, not least because I thought I was going to die from the whooping cough that engulfed me during my stay there. In 1867 the government surveyor, Mr E.A. Delisser, was surveying the land between southern and western Australia and named the place 'Nullus Arbor,' which is Latin for 'No trees'. It's a lovely name but I believe quite irrelevant as there are more than a few trees around now. Those cliffs have to be seen to be believed; they are meant to be the longest cliffs in the world and have a sheer drop of 100 metres. There are no safety railings whatsoever and therefore absolutely nothing to prevent you from falling to your death on the rocks below should you accidentally trip up or lose your footing on a windy day.

The honeymoon didn't end in a proper marriage. I thrived during those years of travelling around Australia under the guidance and care of Peter but I knew in my heart that he and his desires weren't enough for me. Spending the rest of my life with him wasn't an option and gently we went our separate ways. I needed to keep moving, to help people. I'm glad to say that we're still friends today and regularly keep in touch. After the uranium mine I headed back home to Melbourne. I had kept in touch with my family by phone and was looking forward to seeing them again. If the truth be known, I had also missed Melbourne, which will always be, I think, my favourite place in Australia. I was 19 years old and ready to settle down in one place for a bit. I moved in with my friend Rose and her toddler son.

Rose is ten years older than me and remains one of my closest friends. She's slim and attractive with long brown hair. I literally don't remember not knowing her. She is one of those friends who will support you with everything they have, but if you're going off the rails they are the first ones to level with you right between the eyes. She was always great fun and I admired her constant creativity in the different forms it took, from writing to photography. We studied pottery, drank lots of cheap red wine, ate pounds of chocolate cake and spent hours upon hours in deep conversation about men and such like. I fell for her little son and was like a surrogate mother to him. I even loved her mother, a retired teacher and widow who still sends me money today.

Rose and I also worked hard together doing things from putting on puppet shows for kids, to visiting the elderly and helping out the disabled. Helping people was my drug of choice now. I had buckets of energy and good cheer and I loved using it to improve, however briefly, the lives of those I came into contact with.

***

Fast forward to me standing on a crowded busy main street at lunch-hour. I was in downtown Melbourne, which was full of offices and busy people dressed in suits, handing out Christian pamphlets to the mostly male passers-by. Normally they wouldn't have given someone in my position a second glance but I took advantage of my looks. I was a slim, attractive blonde who was dressed reasonably sexily, so I got more attention than most. The men were curious to see what I was handing out and many of them offered some chit-chat. I wasn't shy either and was bouncing up to them saying, 'Hi, how are you? Here's something you might find interesting.'

I became slowly aware that I was being watched by a man. He was gorgeous, and very, very cool. He was leaning in the doorway of a men's clothing store and evenly met my glance. 'Hmm,' I thought and made my way over to him. I handed him a pamphlet and we started to talk. He could have been a model, he was that good-looking. He was also lost and looking for direction, just like I had been. We held an intense discussion in the doorway, I summarised my life to date for him, and we kicked over this need to search for meaning and purpose. Suddenly he had an idea.

'You've got to come with me!'

So I did.

'My friend is opening a high class nightclub and you would be great for the customers.'

'Ok, cool,' I said as I toddled after him down a dark alley and through an open door. I found myself standing in the foyer of a big nightclub called Sheiks. The owner was there and there was a real buzz in the air as the club was to open that night, launched by the American singer George Benson. My new friend marched me up to George the owner, who glanced approvingly at my appearance. The interview was brief; 'Have you got nice legs?'

I lifted my skirt a little.

'Good. You're hired. Go over to that girl with the dark hair and tell her to measure you for your costume.'

I was now a Christian playboy bunny no less; it fitted in perfectly with my plan and personality. The guy I'd spoken to had seen how easily I managed to talk to people and connect with them, and between us we knew that I could continue to talk about Christianity with the customers, allowing them to open up, but in an environment where they didn't feel like they were being judged. For me, it was perfect. I could talk to people who needed help and assurance, and guidance in life, but I could also have some fun while doing it.

I informed my new boss that I wanted to work the quiet nights only. He was surprised and pointed out that it would mean less tips. I shrugged and said that I wanted to talk to people. I also asked to work the lounge, which was the quietest room in the club, where the music was soft and the emphasis was on relaxing and intimate chat. The front of the club was more of a disco with a DJ, bright lights and mirror balls hanging from the ceiling. I worked two set nights, Sunday and Monday, but I would help out if they were stuck for staff. I ended up doing a lot more than serving drinks. I filled in for the receptionist, the hostess, and I even worked in the kitchen when necessary. I really enjoyed it. It suited me because I had decided that I wanted to help people who were lost and lonely. There was no point sitting in a church, since no one, especially the young and successful, go there, but they would go out for a drink, in search of company, preferably female. It was perfect! They would ask me what I did in the day time, probably assuming that I was a student. When I told them about my Christian beliefs and doings, they were amazed and would give me a tip or a kiss. More importantly, they would listen to my message.

There was one customer in particular, a slim, good-looking, well-off executive who was always flanked by different girls every night he came in. He was a bit of a charmer and was always generous with his tips. He would brag to me about his desk in his office creaking under the weight of all his different technical toys and gadgets but I saw through his brashness and believed him to be a lonely guy appalled by the emptiness of his life. He was always ready to chat to me but never quite dropped his guard. I'd like to think that he eventually fell in love with a decent girl and married her and had lots of kids. He actually gave me a generous donation when I left Australia.

There was another guy, Tony, a fat/cuddly Italian who also had lots of money but had been dragged through a bad divorce. He would often search me out to talk about his life, his big house which was too big for him now that he was alone. He went out on lots of dates with these tiny, attractive women, but it was probably too soon after the breakdown of his marriage, and nothing came of them.

I loved my bunny uniform with the big ears and fluffy tail. I would shake my tush and talk about the voluntary mission work I was doing. I was a hit with the staff and clients, and I thrived in this environment. There were lots of conversations with people who wanted more from their life. I listened and counselled and served the cocktails. Sheiks proved a popular spot. It gained relative fame when celebrities, Australian and otherwise, would visit to help promote the club and would end up on the evening news. There was huge controversy when a well-known penthouse model joined the staff as a bunny girl. She may have looked the part but we were forever cleaning up after her; she frequently dropped trays of glasses—full and empty—on the floor or else she would accidentally tip someone's drink into their lap. Anyone else would have been fired, but not a penthouse model!

Staff from nearby nightclubs would come to ours on their nights off and would furnish us with free passes to their place of employment. I made a lot of new friends and danced in a lot of nightclubs aided by free drinks. I even dated the Scottish DJ for a while—I loved his accent. For six months I had a ball and lived day to day without plan or ambition. I felt relatively fulfilled and at peace with myself—relatively.

***

I was alone at the beach one night watching the moonlight shimmer on the water. I don't think I was especially thinking or pondering over anything in particular but suddenly I felt the hairs go up on the back of my neck and I was filled with a buzzing energy. You don't have to believe me but I clearly heard a voice inside my head ask, 'Why are you giving to those who have so much when there are so many who have nothing?'

If I thought the universe was going to praise me for my good works to date—getting people interested in charity work, encouraging them to open up and discuss their problems and worries, and telling them about Christian spirituality—I was brought back down to earth with a bang. I sat there a little stunned, replaying the message in my head until it hit me like Newton's apple; I should go where there are people who have nothing, and I decided:

'Asia!, I'll go to Asia.'

I was quite cold by the time I dragged myself off the damp sand but I also had a date to work towards—11 September, which was a mere three months away. I had no idea how I was going to get to Asia and I certainly had no money, but I wasn't going to worry about that for now. The first thing I did was head to the nightclub to inform my boss at Sheiks that I would be quitting in the near future. I found him downstairs with some of the management staff. He beamed at me when he saw me approach.

'Hey you! We have been talking about you and have just decided we wanted to offer you the position of manager.'

How many times does that happen? You make a big decision to change your life and someone promptly offers to improve the life you have.

'We want to give you more responsibility because you have proved yourself an exemplary employee after six months,' he continued, before I could reply.

I found myself carried along in their excitement and smiled and nodded vacuously while my insides were squirming.

'There is one problem Susan, which I've been meaning to tackle you about.'

He had me curious now, as I fully concurred that I was an exemplary employee.

'We're getting a reputation of being a church, so I'm going to have to ask you to stop talking religion with the customers.'

The cheek of him, I thought. I hadn't preached in ages. Well, the decision was made for me, so I told him:

'Thank you for your kind offer but I'm afraid that I was actually coming down to tell you that I would be leaving. I'm going away in September.'

And that was that.

The people in work were a bit funny about my decision. I think the managers were genuinely disappointed that I was leaving, because I would have made an excellent manager. No one congratulated me on my momentous decision to travel to Asia to help people. In fact it would be safe to describe the general reaction as slightly defensive, as if by saying, 'I'm going abroad to help the less privileged,' was my way of saying, 'Look at you, you're overly-privileged and you don't help anyone,' which I most definitely wasn't saying. It was a strange time.

***

Now that I had made my decision, how was I going to get myself to Asia? I lay in bed and went through a few scenarios for making the money for the air fare. One of my favourite customers at the nightclub floated into my mind's eye. Bingo! I would ask him for the money. Philip was a well-to-do Chinese-Malaysian professor who owned a nightclub and restaurant and drove an expensive Jaguar. We had enjoyed many a deep discussion over the bar. He had gone through a bad divorce and was missing his young son. After two weeks of talking to him he broke down one night in the bar and asked me to pray that he would discover the meaning of his life and what he was meant to do next. I liked him and felt sure that he would support my venture. I don't usually like to ask people for help or money but this was different. The very next evening I walked into the lounge and found the professor at his favourite table. He smiled at me in welcome. I gathered myself together and headed over. I would just be upfront and not bother with the small talk.

'Hiya, guess what? I'm off to Malaysia to do good things and God told me that you would pay for my plane ticket.'

He looked at me to see if I was joking. I trembled a little and he said, 'Oh, I see! Right! Well let's talk about this, why don't you sit down.'

He ordered a bottle of Champagne and we talked until 4am. I told him my entire life story, including the drinking, drugging and rock 'n' rolling. He listened gravely without interrupting me once. Then he asked me why I wanted to go to Asia and what my plan was. He seemed very touched and asked me to let him think about it. He came back to me the next day, and said:

'I feel that you have been completely honest with me and for that you have my trust. So, yes I will buy you your ticket.'

I flung my arms around him in thanks and relief. Now I could start to make my preparations. I was definitely going. Oh my sweet Jesus!

My parents were determined to hear me out and only raise valid, mature points about this new direction of mine. They knew very little about Asia and worried that I could end up being mowed down by a herd of raging, stampeding elephants or drink dirty water or fall out of the tree-house that I might be living in. Their biggest concern was what would happen to me if I fell ill; was there adequate medical treatment available? Philip did me another great favour in agreeing to visit them and explain to them what I could expect in his neck of the woods. They were very taken with his genteel ways and the fact that he was also a parent. He assured them that it was easier, and much cheaper, to get a doctor in Asia than it was in Australia; and that all the latest treatment was widely available. His visit had the desired effect and they were a lot easier in their minds about my going. I was always completely up front with them. I told them that this was something that I had to do and that I was prepared to give it three months. If it didn't work out by then I would be happy to return.

So Philip was buying my air ticket but I still needed money for everything else. I decided to do a little personal fund-raising and approached both everyone I knew and strangers on the street holding up an empty coffee can that I needed filled with coins. Folks were fascinated by my story—that I was going to be a missionary in Asia. I suppose I really didn't look the part and I was still very young of course. I bought a one way ticket, which shocked my family and friends, but that's the cockiness of youth. I had complete faith that things were going to work out just fine! Maybe the excitement had me run ragged but I managed to come down with bronchitis with only a few weeks or so before my flight. My parents eyed me anxiously as I coughed and hacked my way through my final preparations. However, absolutely nothing was going to stop me getting on that plane. They took me out for a lovely dinner the night before I left and made me a present of much-needed cash. Rose was there too, almost as excited for me as I was.

Inevitably I didn't sleep much that night despite the glasses of wine I drank to help me relax. The morning finally came round and I tried to savour my last hours in Melbourne, Australia. I remember eating a particularly gorgeous apple, and wondering how soon it would be before I would taste an apple that good again. On the way to the airport I constantly checked and rechecked all my bits and pieces. I must have worn a hole in my passport with the amount of times I frantically rifled through my holdall, even though I had just held it between my fingers seconds earlier. I clutched it, let it go and immediately fumbled around again as if it might vanish if I couldn't feel it. Rose, her mother, her son, my parents and Annabel saw me off. I didn't cry when I said goodbye because I was so tremendously excited.

I packed just one bag, wanting to keep it simple. Philip was flying out with me. We were landing in Kuala Lumpur where I was to spend a week before moving on to Penang. As usual I was taking a huge risk. Philip was heading on to Hong

Kong to attend to some business dealings while I was going to wait for a miracle with my one bag and very little money. The last I heard of him was that he had married again, to a Filipino, and had settled down in Singapore. Meanwhile, I had a phone number of a guy I had met ages ago in Sydney. I knew he had married a Malay woman and was living and teaching somewhere in Malaysia.

***

The airport in Kuala Lumpur was a tin shed—nothing like its hugeness and variety of shops and restaurants today. When I stepped off the plane I nearly buckled under the immense wall of heat that seemed to descend on us; the typical reaction of westerners to tropical countries. We headed across the tarmac in the middle of the night. I was exhausted but on a high, hardly believing where I was. There were small crowds of youths standing around in groups; I marvelled at the amount of young boys out so late and hanging around an airport. I mentioned this to Philip, who laughed and told me that these were full-grown men and the reason they were 'hanging out' at the airport was because they were taxi drivers waiting to earn a living to feed their families. I looked again. They were shorter, slimmer and much younger looking than the men who drove taxis in Melbourne. They were also mostly dressed the same, stuck in the fashions of the 1970s, with colourful bell-bottomed pants and wide flashy belts. This was the 1980s now but I felt a jolt of nostalgia for the not-so-good old days.

I learned pretty quickly that transparent clothes were going to have to take a back seat in my daily attire. The first morning I innocently went walking in Kuala Lumpur clad in clothes which were normal in Melbourne. I was wearing bright pink shorts and a yellow see-through singlet, and as was usual for me I wasn't wearing a bra. I almost caused a traffic accident. People were almost hanging out of their cars with lolling tongues and gawping eyes, and that was just the women. There were beeping horns, with people whispering and gesturing in my direction. I felt visually mauled and ran back in tears to the safety of the hotel. If that is what being a celebrity is like I'll stop envying Madonna right now! I was so ignorant it actually took me a while to work out that there was nothing wrong with these people. I was the one at fault for dressing inappropriately and walking around a Muslim town. I was utterly shocked and thought about getting on the next plane home. Although, in my defence I would like to point out that I was very young and had spent the previous six months dressed as a playboy bunny!

The second morning I dressed in a cotton t-shirt and hippie skirt and headed out into the hot sun to explore again. I found some markets and bought myself a sarong kabaya, which is the national Malaysian costume. They cover most of the body but are quite tight-fitting so I felt sexy and conservative simultaneously. I received a much friendlier reaction, and people seemed to appreciate my attempt to fit in and conform.

I was to get a lot of early lessons in the customs and behaviour of others too. I walked along the busy street and spotted a family coming towards me. The husband was a huge man, Indian, with three chins and the body of a beached whale. He strode along, nose in the air, oblivious to his nearest and dearest tottering after him. His wife almost matched him in girth and I couldn't help wondering about the possible size of their daily meals and the price of their grocery shopping. Three very young children ran to keep up with their mammoth parents. I got ready to smile dotingly at them but something terrible happened. The father began to make this awful hawking noise, preparing to either vomit or spit. I physically recoiled but couldn't stop watching him. He hawked and hawked until he had collected every last drip of mucus from his vast interior and then he gathered himself to his full height and spat with considerable force. It landed on my left foot, which was only partially covered by my sandal. I screamed at the top of my lungs in horror and disgust. The entire family stared at me, shocked at my behaviour! I can laugh now, but I thought I was going to be sick right there in front of them. He never apologised or acknowledged his glob on my foot.

In Asia this sort of expelling of unwanted body fluids is perfectly normal. It's funny because in Thailand you can openly and diligently pick your nose and ears without bringing any attention on yourself, but just don't put a toothpick to work in your mouth or you'll upset your neighbours. A friend of mine who went to China told me about watching these gorgeous looking girls picking their noses and belching in public but they would never allow themselves to wear a skimpy bikini at the beach because it's not suitable behaviour for a young lady! Then there's Songkla in Thailand where the men walk around in their colourful sarongs that make it easy for them to answer the call of nature—honestly, they just lift their sarong and wee, no matter where they are or who is around them. Of course if a woman was to squat on the street she would be arrested. Typical!

I rang my friend Ben's phone number and was delighted when he answered. He thought that Pete was with me as the last time he saw us was when we were a loved-up couple enjoying the many sites of Sydney. I briefly summarised my life to date for him and he promptly invited me out to his house to have dinner with himself and his wife. Once again God was looking after me. Ben and his lovely wife, Esther, were thinking about moving to Penang; I couldn't believe how serendipity was working for me. A bond was struck between us that day and we decided that not only would I move with them to Penang, but I would also move in with them to share the rent. Esther was gorgeous, with long, black hair, dark skin and always had a smile on her face. She made me feel right at home, with her generous, cheerful nature, and she also spoke very good English. They were hugely considerate people and mindful of the fact that I knew absolutely no one. The relief in my parents' voices on my first phone call was huge.

***

Penang, or the 'Pearl of the Orient', is the name of an island in the Straits of Malacca. It's also a Malaysian state, located on the north-west coast of the Malaysian peninsular. It's not very big—in fact it's the second smallest state in Malaysia after Perlis. We rented a house in Penang. It was quite a large house which allowed us to sub-let rooms. For a while we had a Chinese girl, a secretary, sharing with us. When she moved on we had a fair few people come and go in her place. As a result the rent was very manageable, even affording us to share the expenses of a battered second-hand car. It was a good place to be thanks to the 2,000 Australian Air Force folk based and living in the area. The Aussies left in 1985 and the site in Butterworth is now home to the Butterworth Regional

Meteorological Office of the Malaysian Meteorological Service of the Royal Malaysian Air Force.

We lived very simply. I received small gifts of money and donations from my family and friends in Australia. Then when my visa ran out I would fly to Singapore and do a bit of fund-raising there. The locals were very generous and always liked to give a donation towards whatever project I was working on.

I worked hard in Penang. I had brought puppets over from Australia and Ben and I frequently put on shows for kids. We also set up a service to help out the disabled people in our area. I wanted to learn the Malay language because I hoped to get into one-on-one counselling. However, it quickly became apparent that I wouldn't be using it much as everyone I came in contact with was actually Chinese, or Chinese-Malaysian. It made more sense to learn Hokkien, which is the Chinese language—or dialect—of the Hoklo, an ethnic-cultural group that originated in Fujian. People marvelled at my speed at picking up the language, but as far as I was concerned, my becoming fluent in a short amount of time just proved to me that I was meant to be in Asia; it was where I belonged. In fact I'd go further and say that I was predestined to live here. The Thais would say I must have been Asian in a previous life.

There are large numbers of Hokkien descendants in Malaysia, Singapore, Indonesia, the Philippines, Taiwan and Thailand. I know this because I think I've met most of them! Our Chinese house-mate introduced us to all her friends and then they took us out at night to meet other people. The Chinese are a friendly, curious bunch and make it extremely easy for you to chat them up at the local food stalls. These stalls are great meeting places at night and the food is good too. They're not afraid to ask questions, and I love to talk, so we were perfect for each other. Also, the fact that I was Australian was a big plus; because of the Australian Air Force base Aussie dollars were very popular. I was meeting quite a lot of disenchanted young Chinese people and ended up giving quite a few impromptu counselling sessions alongside learning Hokkien and Mandarin Chinese. I enjoyed these people and even today I would probably be more suited to the Chinese personality than the Malay. The Chinese are just more direct; you always know where you are with them. No matter where I have travelled to I always end up meeting Chinese people. When I went to Indonesia a few months later I ended up counselling wealthy Chinese people. They were very open with me, perhaps because I was an independent foreigner who wanted and needed nothing from them.

I stayed in Penang for a year or so. I would have to leave every so often for another place, like Songkla, because I hadn't got a long term visa, so I would need to leave to get my passport stamped elsewhere. There was nothing grand or routine about our work. I wasn't interested in getting involved and working through organised Christian groups or churches—they were too bureaucratic and narrow-minded for me and spent a lot of time debating denominational theories. Instead, I worked very informally: for instance one day I got a very strong feeling that I should go to the beach—Penang has the most fabulous beaches—and when I got there I got chatting to this Chinese guy who was utterly fed up with himself and his life. After a couple of hours in conversation I challenged him to come and help me out for a bit with my work, which he duly accepted, taking his mind off his problems and making him feel a whole lot better. Another time I got on a bus and happened to sit next to a woman who was practically suicidal. I got off the bus with her and we went for a coffee, over which we talked until she too felt better. This type of one-on-one work is perfect for helping me to assimilate myself into the culture of the country I'm working in. It's like a backdoor in, which allows me to skip over months of trying to learn the ins and outs of that particular society.

Now you can call it what you will: woman's intuition, something supernatural, a Guardian Angel or just plain weird, but this is how I have built up my career. I follow my inner voice, which always directs me to someone in need. One Sunday I headed into town and had the feeling that I should go into a hotel that I liked to have coffee in from time to time. It had a swimming pool but you had to be a paying guest of the hotel in order to be able to use it so I sent a little prayer upwards that I might be given permission to use it at some stage. I love to swim; it's an excellent way to de-stress yourself. I went into the bar because, as with in many walks of life, that seemed the best place to start. There were a few people around reading newspapers or engaged in intimate chats. I took a table and ordered a beer from the waiter. A few minutes later a guy, Malaysian, walked in and took the table behind me. I had a feeling that he could speak English and asked him if he could. He smiled in surprise and said yes, asking me in turn how I could have known. I shrugged and said quite truthfully that I just had a feeling he did. He looked me directly in the eye and said, 'I think God must have sent you here.'

I was delighted and replied, 'And you too.'

We ended up having dinner and a few more drinks. He was a journalist with a local newspaper and wrote a political column. It was a very enjoyable evening and one I wasn't to forget about quickly since he left my name at the swimming pool, which meant I could use it whenever I liked. So you see why I believe in miracles!

***

Once I stopped wearing transparent clothes I felt very at home in Asia. I adored the food especially. I developed a reputation for being able to eat an entire jar—and not suffer from any diarrhoea—of Sambal Blachan, which is a really smelly chilli paste made from shrimps. It's only supposed to accompany meat, fish or rice but I just eat it by itself, straight from the jar. I also relish Beef Randang and a fried chicken dish called Nasi Goreng but I'm ashamed to say that the nicest meat dish I ever had was frog. They told me it was chicken, but it wasn't, it was frog, and it must have been a big one because it was a fair sized chunk of meat. However, I'm not completely foolhardy about what I put it my mouth. I attended a Chinese business meeting once and refused to taste the main course, which was 10,000 Singaporean dollars, of seal's penis and testicle stew. I could think of so many other ways to spend that kind of money. I also draw the line at eating turtle's feet. Those majestic massive creatures always remind me of dolphins; they look like they have a soul and intellect—it's hard to feel the same way about a chicken.

I kept in frequent contact with home through letters and was thrilled when my parents told me that they were saving to come and visit me. They flew in on a night flight so they were a bit groggy when they got off the plane. Dad couldn't fathom why his glasses were all steamed up, but it was just the heavy heat, even at night time. It was an emotional reunion. For my part I got a bit of a shock at how much they had apparently aged in a year or so, while I looked taller and more grown-up to them. The three of us stayed in a plush 5-star hotel by the seaside. I think whatever worries they had about losing me were dispelled by our taking a holiday together and spending time re-connecting and catching up with one another. They were delighted with my fluency in Chinese and my bargaining skills with the local rickshaw riders. One ancient Chinese guy muttered to my father, 'Uh oh, madam is very tough!'

I have to admit that I had developed a talent for bargaining, and a short time after arriving in Malaysia I was paying the local prices, instead of the inflated 'tourist prices', though when I have the cash I do like to tip, but it's more usually the case that I just can't afford to give 'tourist' amounts.

I had asked my mother to bring me over a list of things that I missed and she duly arrived with liquorice (which I sorely missed), Vegemite (but of course!), and lots of bras and pants. At that time, underwear was really expensive to buy in Asia, except for children of four, or for those huge granny knickers sported by grand old ladies past their prime; they were even bigger—the pants, that is—than the pair Renee Zellweger wears in the movie, *Bridget Jones' Diary*, and they were made from a horrible plastic, nylon material. My poor mother sent me a mountain of cheap, colourful underwear over the years. Fortunately things have improved in that department, and nowadays the underwear that is made in Thailand is also sold, cheaply, in Thailand.

We ate out every night; sometimes we'd go to my kind of place—cheap, greasy with dodgy décor, and we'd also go to their sort of place—quiet, candles, and gorgeous western-Chinese food, which is much different from the local Chinese fare, unless you have a lot of money. I enjoyed a week of good food, beer, wine and swims in the hotel pool.

The weather was glorious and I believed them when they told me that it was the best vacation they had ever had. In hindsight, I think that Asia surprised them with its beauty and its gentle, friendly people. They could see why I loved it. They also didn't feel too isolated thanks to the British bars, restaurants and tourists. I think they might have been hoping to hear me say that I was coming home with them, or in the near future, but to their credit they never said it to me. To this day I know they would love for me to return to Melbourne and get a good, secure job but they also realise that that is probably not going to happen.

***

Some time later I was eager to stretch my wings and move on from Penang. I think I always knew that I would be leaving at some stage and was just waiting to see where I would be directed to. We got a call from a wealthy Chinese guy who was a Christian and was living with his wife in Indonesia. I had met him about a year before and he had generously donated to various causes, which were not my own but which I felt were good investments, spiritually, for him.

He owned quite a few properties and wanted to donate one of them to be set up as a drug rehab centre for the troubled youth in Jakarta. The city had a particularly bad drug problem and its rehab facilities, as in most Asian countries at that time, were dismal to say the least. Drugs could be quite cheap to get; the likes of heroin and gancha were the poor man's drug of choice. The addict was perceived to be the worst kind of loser and the solution, at the time, was to lock him, or her, up in an ugly cell and let them go cold turkey without any help or care. Someone was needed to help set up and run the project.

I jumped at this perfectly timed opportunity and packed my few belongings, ready for a new beginning and a new challenge.

Jakarta wasn't as pleasant a place as Penang. As I've said Penang had the most wonderful beaches, making it the perfect holiday spot, and the people were incredibly friendly. I had always felt very safe there. Jakarta was different; it was a mad house—dirty, polluted and over-populated. It was also, at a moment's notice, a hot bed of rebellion. One time I had to stay holed up in my hotel room while 10,000 people rioted outside my window as a protest against the government. There were a lot of under-privileged, poor people which made it a perfect place for me to do my work and stretch myself.

***

I spent the next few years project-hopping from country to country. As usual I had no particular plan or schedule and just set about being open and available to whoever needed me. I was beginning to make a name for myself; people would ask for me and send me plane tickets so that I could head out for short periods of time, though always within Malaysia. Once again I enjoyed the freedom and independence just like when Pete and I headed around Australia. I did make lots of new friends in the different Christian groups that I came into contact with but I had no real ties and wasn't perturbed by the constant travelling and living alone, or bunking in with assorted friends.

But then I got a call from my friend in Thailand. Richard was working for the army and was given a few passes to the Southeast Asian Games and told to 'bring goodwill' to Thailand. A mutual friend suggested to him that he should ask me to accompany him since I spoke a few of the local languages and got on very well with Asians and would more than likely say yes to coming along.

The Southeast Asian Games is a bi-annual multi-sport event involving the current 11 countries of Southeast Asia. In 1985 the 13th games were being held in Bangkok, from 8–17 December. Richard rang me and begged me to come over and be an interpreter during the games. All along I somehow knew that I would end up in Thailand and the idea didn't appeal to me. Realising your destiny is a two-edged sword in that it is both exhilarating and utterly terrifying. For now I considered his offer.

'Nine days Susan, just nine days out of your life that's all I'm asking for. You'll have a great time, I promise you!'

How could I resist that?

It was great fun. Again there was nothing formal about my role. I just hung out with the athletes and their crews and the media crowd, befriending them and helping out wherever I could. After the nine days were up I was asked —as I knew I would be—why didn't I just stay on for a while? I returned to Indonesia to once again pack up all my belongings. Then I flew to Singapore for a quiet Christmas. I rang my parents before dousing what was probably going to be my last Christmas pudding for a while, in brandy. Afterwards I headed out for a walk along the streets, taking in the bright lights and the hundreds of beaming Singaporeans and Westerners who were out celebrating.

This was it, I knew that my life was about to change forever; Thailand was where I was meant to be; I couldn't deny or resist it any longer.

CHAPTER THREE

One of my first jobs in Thailand was minding Richard's kids. He had recently married his second wife, a Thai woman, and they were expecting their first child together. In the meantime he needed me to look after his four American children from his first marriage. Richard was also a member of a Christian group and managed to do as much voluntary work as he could in between his day-time job as a teacher and his full-time career as a busy father. Naturally, once I had settled in, I helped him out with his charity work whenever I was needed. I hadn't got a long term visa yet and had to keep leaving the country every six months. I would go visit my friends in Penang and Indonesia and help out in any projects that I could.

One of the first projects that I set up on my own was teaching English to the Tourist Police. This branch of the police department was mostly made up of young recruits who had recently joined from up-country provinces. The vast majority had never been in busy Bangkok in their lives, never mind being next to near a tourist, and certainly did not know a word of English; therefore, if some enraged

German or American had been the victim of a pick-pocket it would immediately become an impossible and frustrating situation for both parties. The tourist industry was becoming an increasingly viable and necessary asset to Thailand, so something had to be done. A course, including text books, had been specially written for them at Thammasart University but there was no one available to teach it.

I heard about their dilemma and approached the chief of the Tourist Police to offer my services. He was an interesting guy, with fairer skin than me, and a Clark Gable moustache. He spoke English fluently, having studied in England, and was an advocate of education and learning. He was the one who had initiated the university course and now needed a teacher. I recruited two other women to help and we began teaching classes early in the morning, before the officers' shift.

It was a great experience for me, and it also got me my visa, which enabled me to stay and work in Thailand. In fact, on my first visit to the immigration office I was transported in a Tourist Police car, with two young guards in full uniform. I was in the back seat with two girlfriends; Renee, who would help deliver my baby a few years later, and Julie, who I had known in Australia. I had first met her when I was still a teenager, in the coffee shop of a Christian youth group. We all needed our visas stamped and were thrilled with our ride—more so when we realised that onlookers were staring aghast at us, obviously putting two and two together and thinking we had all been arrested.

I wonder what they thought we had done, since the three of us looked so harmless and polite. It became more comical when we reached the immigration building and our stern young escorts walked us in past the other westerners who were filling out their forms in the crowded office. People either openly stared at us in pity or avoided our eyes in pity; meanwhile, we were being treated better than any of them there.

After some years in Bangkok I was followed by the Secret Police—when they could keep up with me. I was a strange white face who was constantly on the move around the city, and seemed to spend a large amount of time popping into police stations. Was I a spy? Their attitude changed when they discovered that I was quite poor but genuinely happy to spend my day helping others. They called me into their headquarters to ask me if I would also teach them English in exchange for a donation for my purse.

One of the police generals asked me for my help. He wanted to send his son to school in Australia but knew little about the schools available. I agreed to look into and make the required arrangements. Later that week, it just so happened that I had to run into the 5-star hotel, in Siam Square, to use its pristine bathroom. On my way out I spotted a familiar face in the lobby—Mr Ross, one of my teachers from the private school. I couldn't believe it. It's weird enough to see your teachers out in the real world when you're a kid, and it's definitely astonishing to be looking at one in a fancy hotel in Thailand.

He smiled politely at me without recognising me but was obviously wondering why I was grinning insanely in his direction. His mouth dropped open when I introduced myself; I had been a right handful in his class and he had to battle me frequently over who was going to win the other students' attention. I think part of his surprise was that one, I was still alive and two, I didn't have as many facial piercings as I used to. He grabbed my hand warmly when I told him what I was doing with my life;

'Oh my goodness! I'm actually dealing with a girl who reminds me of you. She called me the other day looking for help and I felt I had nothing to give her but now you are living proof that there is hope for her.'

He told me that he was now the principal of a boarding school, just outside Melbourne.

As we chatted, an idea formed in my head and I mentioned the General and his son. He gave me the registrar's phone number and warned me to tell the General to act quickly as there were only a few places left for the next school term. We said our goodbyes and promised to keep in touch. The General had heard of the boarding school and had decided that it would be his first choice. It all worked out beautifully. We made the call and his son got the very last place in the school and at a reduced rate since we had rung the school directly.

I quickly discovered that Thais prefer to know someone. My involvement and the fact that I knew the principal of the school made it a lot easier for the General to enrol his son in a *farang* (foreign) school. It's just the Thai way; you never do something cold with complete strangers; you always do business guided by who you know. It's about security, especially when it comes to their kids, which I completely understand. This meant that not only was the son signed up for the school, but the family wanted me to come to Melbourne with them to settle him in, and also to settle any doubts that might have lingered. The General wouldn't take no for an answer and my ticket was bought for me before I knew it. I was over the moon as it felt like such a long time since I had seen my home town.

I flew into Melbourne with the General's petite wife and their smiling, polite son. It was a culture shock for me. Everyone just seemed so physically big, including their noses, and why were they shouting so much? Asian people are so contained in manner and stature that I had forgotten what your average Aussie was like. When we got into the taxi at the airport I sat in the front so that I could address and direct the taxi man. Up to that point I quite enjoyed having them depend on me and was doing my 'Welcome to my country' thing; my confidence was quickly shook, however, when the cab driver couldn't understand my accent and point blank refused to believe I was as Australian as he was.

Australia had changed a lot since I had been away— including the telephone system and the money. I felt like a foreigner in my own country, visiting it for the very first time. It was strange to see so many white people and I found myself staring at men's beer bellies and the cellulite-dimpled arms and legs of the women. I didn't feel too bad when I caught the General's wife doing the same—and she was much more ladylike than I was.

Money was no object on this trip; the General had us booked into one of Melbourne's downtown hotels. I was being paid to be a chaperone so while I wanted to run off and see my family and friends that would have been rude and unfair, as neither mother nor son had much English and they would have been stranded if I disappeared. My job was to help the son get settled in the little time we had; I knew once he was happy his mother would be happy. Before we left Thailand the General had contacted the abbot of the Thai temple in Melbourne, who was delighted to help out. We met him and his 76-year-old sidekick the following day and they were anxious to show the General's wife and son the sights, and brought the car. It quickly became apparent that they were going to be much better tour guides than myself.

They had been living there for the last ten years and knew all the short cuts and all the different sights that Melbourne had to offer. Everyone thought it was great fun that I was being shown around my hometown by a Thai monk. We were all in good spirits, laughing and joking in Lao and Thai—it was almost like we were on a little Thai island inside the car, watching an Australian movie through the windows.

I was re-united with my family later that day and kept busy fitting in as many visits as I could. I even caught up with my old boyfriend Simon. We bumped into each other on the street. He recognised me first and, like my meeting with Mr Ross, it took me a couple of seconds before I realised who this large, friendly, smiling man was. All his hardness and toughness had fallen away, thanks largely as I discovered, to his lovely wife and three little daughters that he was completely smitten with. He proudly introduced his young family to me and it was heart-warming to see him basking in the warmth and love of all these females. After the teenage anger and then the soul-searching, he was now a man happy in his own skin. I found myself envying him as I too hoped to have children and find that soul-mate that 'they' tell us is out there. Little did I know what the universe had planned for me.

***

On my return to Thailand I threw myself into my work again. I continued with the English classes and my police contacts enabled me to get involved in many different things. I had joined with a Christian group in Bangkok and we were starting to feel a way around to establish where we could focus our energies. Through the Metropolitan Police I became involved in the juvenile welfare department. I spent the next three years as an official instructor of activities and projects organised in conjunction with the police for the youth of Bangkok.

When I started this job there was a lot of trouble on the streets in the form of street battles between the student-gangs of opposing technical schools. I don't quite know how it initiated; it seemed to have become the tradition—a tradition that began years earlier—that if you attended one school you were automatically the enemy of every other technical school in the district. And woe betide if a student of one college, easily recognised because of his school uniform, infringed on the territory of another; punishment was usually instant and vicious, with most of the kids armed with knives or using the buckle of their belts to beat the living daylights out of the opposition. These gangs would take, at the very least, the belt, with the school's crest, of their victims as a kind of trophy to the day's battle. The clashes were becoming increasingly more violent over the years until eventually the inevitable happened; some of the kids got their hands on guns and a student was shot dead. Bangkok was horrified at the turn of events, and something needed to be done.

While I would never describe myself or my Christian colleagues as miracle-workers, we worked hard to stay optimistic and make a difference, small or otherwise. The juvenile division of the police set up a programme in Saraburi, which is a beautiful location about 108km from Bangkok and capital of the Saraburi Province. There was a camp on the grounds of a temple. The police would rent it out to schools and youth groups. They decided it would be perfect for what they had in mind and set about bringing ten students from each of the troublesome schools. It was a bit of a risk but it was worth it. In fact this was just one of several camps set up for this purpose. The students underwent a tough military regime. If they had any ideas about forming mini-armies and inflicting harm on each other that first evening in Saraburi, they didn't follow it through, out of pure exhaustion. They didn't know what had hit them; we had them run blindfold through the forest at night, we had them helping each other to scale barbed wire and once we got the first day out of the way we could start to mix and match up different teams. Inevitably they began to forget about the territorial façade in Bangkok because it just wasn't relevant in the forest in Saraburi. Conversations were, grudgingly at first, struck up, and little by little the kids started working together.

A frequent visitor to these camps was Niall, a volunteer worker and musician, and fellow Aussie. I had met him at a party in a friend's house, in Thailand, a couple of years previously, but we hadn't spoken to one another. He may have perceived me to be this big news voluntary worker and perhaps that scared him off—or perhaps it was my brash behaviour and loud laugh and my complete inability to look shy and enticing. Whatever it was, back then I was happily single and disinterested as far as cute guys who played the guitar were concerned. But now here he was again and this time it was different. He was fluent in Thai, hugely intelligent and creative—always a turn-on for me. He was in great demand as a composer of children's songs, and was busy writing material and putting together Thai educational videos.

A lot of the friends I had were meeting people and falling in love and I'd be lying if I said that I wasn't affected by it. I had been single for a long time at this stage and even though I was 110% committed to my work I was starting to feel lonely and would find myself daydreaming about my soul mate and the father of my future children. At our camp, we would often have meals together, in the company of maybe eight other people. Then, it happened; one evening we found ourselves having dinner alone and thus had our first real conversation ... and suddenly the sparks were flying between us. I felt a shiver creep up my back that I hadn't felt for a long, long time. I suppose it was all inevitable when I think about it—you open yourself up for an experience and when the universe judges you to be ready it's all systems go. We both shared the same goals; to live our lives helping others, and duly fell madly in love. There is simply nothing in life that is as incredible as the start of a relationship. People just take on a radiance when they are falling in love with someone new and the feeling is being reciprocated. I swear I hadn't looked this good in years.

My happiness at this time was increased considerably when I soon found out I was pregnant. I had been dying to have a baby ever since I was a child myself. I guess adopted people never lose that desire to be completely related to someone else, especially, if like myself, the birth parents are never found or they reject you a second time. I knew instantly the moment it happened; it was a beautiful summer's day outside his bedroom window and I knew we had just conceived a child—naturally I didn't tell him that until it was official. We were having dinner with friends on

Valentine's Day and as he passed by me to get his guitar I whispered, 'By the way I'm pregnant!' It was mean of me, I know, but I did get a lot of fun out of watching him trying to act normal for the rest of the evening. He kept sneaking me looks of pure gladness—and, yes, a little shock—but I pretended not to see them, to prolong his agony. My parents were equally thrilled when I rang them with the news. They had met Niall in Thailand and had spoken to him on the phone many times and genuinely liked him.

It is not easy being pregnant during the Thai hot season. I suffered from morning sickness for the first few months but I couldn't afford to rest up since there was so much work to be done. I felt nauseous, bloated, and dizzy, but had to keep going. I was practically living on orange juice full of honey and brewer's yeast, which did help a little. Probably the most upsetting aspect was that I no longer wanted to eat any of my favourite foods; I couldn't even look at a bowl of tomato soup, something I had loved since I was a kid. And as for liquorice—eugh! Thankfully, the second trimester was a lot easier. I was filled with a new energy, my hair was shiny, I was able to exercise and I ate really well for the baby. I felt and looked fabulous, even if I say so myself, despite starting to resemble a large bird with skinny limbs and a big round belly but with an enviable, blonde mane of glossy hair.

After five and a half months I started to work more from home but that doesn't mean I slowed down or started sleeping until mid-day. I did a colossal amount of mail work; I was ministering a large amount of people and was also corresponding daily regarding a spiritual programme I had created, in Thai and English. Up to that point I continued visiting families, patients and drug addicts. I had always been careful about my own safety and hygiene but now I became strident in keeping my work clothes, and shoes, out of the house and would only eat the lunch I prepared for myself.

I had only ever wanted a girl for as long as I could remember, and I fervently hoped and prayed for a daughter. My prayers were duly answered when I underwent a scan and my tentative suspicions were confirmed.

A close friend called Nina was particularly good to me during my pregnancy and always made sure I ate well. She was originally from Bangkok but had been living in Changmai. She had recently returned to her home town and was sharing with some friends I knew. Then she ended up moving in to the big house with Niall, me and the other members. She was also a very devoted aid worker and was with me on many projects.

In the last few months she went that extra mile and made my breakfast every morning—cheese, egg and chilli on toast—absolutely delicious. I was also eating, in the third trimester, lots of home-made, healthy, peanut balls that were full of yeast, honey and milk powder. Although I wouldn't like to know exactly how many calories there are in one I can heartily recommend them for their nutrients and nourishment. I put on about 18kg, which was fine by me. When I was at eight months, the doctors worried that I was too small to carry, and deliver, a full-term baby so I determined not to worry about calories or extra pounds. Anyway, I lost 11lb giving birth and the rest of the weight seemed to head to my breasts to feed the baby; I was like Dolly Parton for a few all-too-short months.

***

I had never really given much thought to the labour itself; it's inevitable there will be one at the end of the nine months but you don't need, or particularly want, to dwell on it. Anyway, I met lots of supportive, positive mothers, who reminded me that it would all be worth it in the end, and it's not as bad as 'they' say, and that was good enough for me. I mean, I was vaguely aware that I wasn't being told the full truth but I suppose it's like an unspoken conspiracy so that first-time mothers don't go out of their mind with worry.

She arrived a week early; it was 7.23am on the morning of Monday, 1 October when I gave birth to my beautiful little girl. She was 7.7lbs and I was in tears at the perfection of this little thing that had finally come out of me. I was going crazy and danced myself into labour on the Friday; that's right, I actually danced like a mad woman demented by the full moon, with the intention of bringing on the labour early. Friday's contractions disappeared all day Saturday before finally resuming on Sunday, whereupon they grew in size over the next 24 hours.

Things were happening at a snail's pace on the Sunday evening but I refused to take anything to speed up the process. I had decided that I wanted a completely natural birth because I have always believed that that is the best thing for the baby. Perhaps it was still a throw back to my own birth and rejection but I wanted to be fully conscious and ready to welcome her the second she was out. My birth coach, Renee, had been preparing me for weeks on my breathing. During my early labour, she almost got left behind when I spent five hours speed walking around the hospital in order to outrun the contractions. I had really bad back pain, which I hadn't expected, so I just kept moving because it hurt too much to stay still. This strength just flooded my

body and I felt like running a marathon, at least until the
bad contractions kicked in. I also didn't want to be tied
up in stirrups or even wear a hospital gown so I remained
free and naked the whole time. Fortunately, the dear Thai
attendant did an internal check to see how dilated I was and
it turned out I wasn't at all. She didn't tell me this and instead
sneaked in a bone-coloured crochet hook—well, that's what
it looked like to me—punctured the water-bag and whoosh,
it was like a geyser. It was also a wonderful relief since the
sudden gushing and pouring sped up the contractions and I
immediately started to dilate rapidly.

When she finally arrived it was a bit frightening at first
because she was blue and didn't appear to be breathing. The
chord had wrapped itself around her neck twice. Meanwhile,
I nearly died myself when the doctor stuck his hand into me
to fish around for some of the placenta that was refusing
to come out. I screamed and screamed, and actually had
my first non-drug-induced out of body experience. He
was fortunate I was too weak to avenge my poor, wrecked
vagina. I completely understood why women used to go
off alone into the jungle or bush, dig a hole and just hang
on to a stick or pole for support. My face was bruised from
three hours of almighty pushing on my part but I can tell
you truthfully that it was the best experience I have ever had
on this planet. I bawled when she came out and immediately
wanted another. It was utterly exhilarating. The pain, the
tearing and the blood—I instantly wiped it clean from my
mind at the sight of her.

Niall had spent the labour just outside the door, praying
in the corridor. I knew he wouldn't have the stomach to
watch the delivery and didn't want to be worrying about
him as well as myself and the baby. During one of my speed-

walking jaunts I ordered a breathless Renee to go and tell him to comb his hair because it was driving me absolutely nuts. It was comforting to find that my obsessive compulsive behaviour wasn't intimidated by my being in labour! At one stage he fell asleep and I sent Renee out there to wake him up and inform him that he had better stay awake and keep praying. If I could have gone out myself I would have, if only to put the fear of God into him. Honestly, it was bad enough that he couldn't physically share in the agony but I sure wasn't going to have him blissfully asleep either.

He finally got to do his bit when they had to knock me out to retrieve that last piece of missing placenta. Renee remained with me while Niall took my newborn daughter Talya in his arms and sang to her.

***

A couple of days later, I was able to bring her home. It wasn't easy for those first couple of months. I was working again—mad, I know—and the rest of the time I was either expressing milk or breast-feeding. Naturally, I managed to wear myself out and ended up having to use the bottle for Talya after I came down with several fevers and breast infections. I was anxious to get on with my life and be a mom and I think this happens to a lot of first-time mothers. The shock of labour is huge and can take a while to come to terms with; I don't think I was fully right until a year after the birth. But there is another shock in store that isn't as widely promoted as the pain of childbirth and that is the simple fact that having a baby is utterly life-changing. Some women, and I was one of them, believe that they can continue on with their previous life and goals, and that the baby won't change them at all.

I'm here to tell you that you may be able to control your man, your mother and even your best friend, but you cannot control a newborn baby.

All of my friends rallied around us when we got home. There was cake, 'Welcome Home' banners and lots of touching cards. Talya's Thai godparents gave her a beautiful set of gold anklets that had bells on them so you could hear your baby kick when it was awake and later when it was older and discovering the joys of being mobile you could locate it by the tinkle of the little bells. Gold is a typical Asian gift; it's perceived to be a practical and meaningful gift. The gold anklets proved to be extremely practical when, as a pre-teen, Talya cashed them in and was able to get herself lots of goodies like clothes and cds.

I was more tired than I ever remember. I was getting up at 4.30am to wash nappies between the early and late morning feeds. Then when she slept I would feverishly work until she woke. It never occurred to me to take it easy. I wish now that I hadn't worked so much up to the birth. It would have been an act of supreme kindness if I had allowed myself to rest up for a couple of weeks before the birth; it would also have been completely out of character! Besides when I watched her learn to recognise my voice and then my face, and then learn to smile, I felt utterly rewarded.

When she was nine months old and the most bonny baby you could ever meet, my delighted parents came out to see her. It was the start of a beautiful relationship between them. It was thanks to my mother's present of a baby name's book during my pregnancy that I saw the name Talya, which was Hebrew and meant 'gentle dew from Heaven'. To me she looked like a bean sprout or *tua-ngok*, as I used to call her in Thai, because she was so long and skinny. It was funny when

I explained to one of my friends, a Singaporean doctor, what Talya meant and he thought I was saying 'gentile Jew from Heaven.'

Niall was also busy with his work and friends urged me to support him in every way and not distract him from it, and I didn't question their advice—advice which I find strange and intrusive now. He had a genuine love for people and believed in the healing, soothing power of music. He was passionate and ambitious about his work, as I was about mine, but maybe it's true, that whole thing about women being better at multi-tasking. We can do our jobs and also keep working at our love life. For me I felt the romance fading quietly from the relationship and wanted to make the break before he did. We had made this one perfect thing, our daughter, and I felt that this was going to be as good as it was ever going to get, and I wanted more for me.

I wanted a life-long mate who was going to support me 100%, and need and respect, me and that just wasn't happening anymore with us. It's all a bit vague now when I look back and I feel that things might have been different had we been more open with one another. I felt disappointed that he didn't fight more for us, but why would he when it looked like I had already made up my mind to separate from him? I had already been the pushy and aggressive one so why did I think he was going to change now? As far as I saw it, his work was more important and more fulfilling to him than I could ever be and I found myself wondering if I should release him to it.

We were so busy with our individual projects, and then I had Talya to feed, that I wasn't able to defend our relationship and potential future against the doubts of my friends. A couple of our mutual friends sat me down for three hours one night and, in no uncertain terms, warned me that he would break my heart. Whether they were right or not I'll never know because I wasn't prepared to take the risk, but it would be wrong of me to blame them for my decision. At the end of the day I felt I wasn't getting all that I wanted, and needed, so I cut my losses and moved on.

Ten years after we parted I found out that he had actually wanted us to stay together; he just never said it to me—though maybe I never asked. I've never been entirely confident that I made the right decision in breaking with him, but there is no point in dwelling on the 'ifs' and 'might have beens'. We have always maintained a good friendship and he will always be Talya's dad. Enough said.

CHAPTER FOUR

I wanted to start doing personal counselling at the hospitals in Bangkok because as with everything else I had been doing, I wanted to help those most in need. Our first big visit was to the Police Hospital and involved a Police General we knew who had cancer. One of his nephews was a friend of ours and he rang to ask would we go in. I went in with other volunteers; Nina, Michael, and one of my best friends, Maria. It wasn't an easy visit to make since the General's entire family were gathered in the room and most of them were clearly in a distressed state. I had to stifle a gasp when I saw the patient in his bed; he was just a skeleton after losing 80lbs. He had been diagnosed with cancer a few years before and, up to that point, had put up a brave fight. Now, however, he was slowly dying, but neither he nor his relatives had acknowledged it aloud. The room was full of tension and tears and I sensed what was needed was words.

He hadn't lived an overly good life and had been trying to make amends for this during the last year. In fact he was reputed to have been quite a brutal man in his job, and owned up to years of torturing prisoners in order to extract confessions. His past plagued his sickness and made him afraid of being inflicted with eternal punishment beyond the grave. We had actually accompanied him when he started to do 'good acts', like giving money to poor students; he set up funding schemes for schools, and he also made merit at temples. Making a merit is basically giving a gift to the temple in order to be forgiven for bad actions.

He beckoned the four of us to his bed while the family respectfully hung back. He was struggling to speak and looked to me like a man who knew he hadn't got long. I took his hand in mine and Nina drew near to hear him so that she could translate. Breathless with the effort, he openly conveyed his fears for what lay ahead for him after all the evil acts he had performed as Police General. The fear was the only thing keeping him alive; his poor wasted body looked like it was finished. I looked into his eyes, and said: 'General, you need to let go now, it's time. You have nothing to be scared about, so just lay down your worries. You are free from all sin now and you have asked for forgiveness. Ahead of you are your loved ones that are waiting to greet you.'

I felt everyone in the room, including the General, being released from the strain of not mentioning death. The worst had been said now, and there was no going back. The family were free now to say their personal goodbyes and he was free to accept them. He wept silently, knowing, at last, that this was it. We left soon after and I was thankful to return the smile he gave me as we left the room. Our friend rang us the next day to tell us that, within minutes of us leaving, the General had asked for the drip to be removed from his arm and went peacefully in his sleep a few hours later. He thanked us profusely on behalf of the family. It must be so hard to see a loved one weakening in front of your eyes, but how much worse is it if the person is fighting the inevitable in pure terror and won't allow any talk about what is happening. The family's gratitude was inspiring as I felt we had truly made a huge difference, but there were many more cases like this.

As a result, Nina and I paid a visit to the head of the Police Hospital, Dr Gomin, and asked for his permission to start visiting all the wards in the hospital, spending time with patients and doing errands for them. There is probably more genuine praying going on in hospitals than in any church or temple. If you have never prayed in your life and you are suddenly faced with your dwindling mortality or that of a loved one's in a hospital room, my guess is that you find yourself breaking the habit of a lifetime.

It can be particularly difficult for Thai nurses and doctors since they just don't know how to be direct; they are almost repressed by their politeness and wouldn't know how to break the news to someone that they are dying, or even that they would have to take away a part of your intestine, for example. The doctor understood this and gladly gave us permission to set up our visitation programme. I heard a lot of strange stories from the patients—all of them from the police force—about how they received their injuries and what effect their experience had on them. One highway policeman had his arm ripped right off in a hit and run. He managed to get up and headed towards a main road to look for help. He tried to flag down help, including a low-flying helicopter, by waving his bloody arm, but it must have proved too gruesome a sight and it was quite a while before someone stopped to help him. The people who picked him up drove to their nearby home to fetch a cooler into which they placed the severed limb, and then they drove full speed to the hospital. However, when the medical team prepared to attach the arm they discovered that it was completely frozen and all the nerves were dead—it was, therefore, useless.

***

Most of the staff in the hospital quickly assessed how much help we could be to them and freely availed of our assistance. One policeman was brought in after shooting himself in the head during a drunken game of Russian Roulette. He lay quietly in his bed with a massive bandage around his head. He was going to be blind but the nurses didn't want to tell him, so they asked us to. I dreaded telling a young, healthy man that his sight was gone for good; however, as it turned out, he already knew it himself but was glad to have it confirmed aloud for him. It was worse not knowing, and the staff avoiding his nervous inquiries.

Every time I walked on to the wards there were different stories to hear and deal with. There was one guy who had got lost in a large forest and contracted malaria. His brain was mad with fever and it appeared that he had lost his mind. He lay comatose and didn't seem to even be breathing. Nina and I spent time with him and talked gently to him, even if it looked like he was beyond this world. Months later when he had recovered somewhat, he thanked us for our care and assured us that he heard every word that we said, but that he couldn't react because the sickness had a grip on his mind.

Some of the staff gave us some attitude. The first time we entered the therapy ward I went up to the ward sister and said, 'Hi, we have permission from Dr Gomin to visit the patients and help you and them out in any way we can.'

Maybe she was having a bad day but she looked me up and down—and not in a good way—before sulkily muttering, 'Yeah right!'

Obviously she preferred to take the attitude that I had dared to go above her head and, therefore, undermine her despite the fact that this was the first time we had met. I continued to smile as innocently as I could until she grudgingly gestured towards a patient behind me.

'Well start with him then. He was shot in the back and is now paralysed from the waist down. Only be careful, he's very aggressive. In fact he's so aggressive that none of the nurses will go near him. Good luck with that!'

She turned away and marched off, leaving me and Nina to glance at one another before turning to face the problem patient. I took a deep breath and decided to jump right in before thinking about it for too long. He was staring straight ahead when I approached him.

'Hi, what happened to you? The nurse says you were shot?'

He muttered something inaudible and continued staring away from me. Nina gave me a, 'Keep going, you're doing just great,' smile.

'Listen mate, if you don't look at me this very minute and give me a damn smile I'm going to jump on top of you and tickle you until you cry!'

That got his attention. He stared at me in shock, with, perhaps, just a tiny hint of fear. Since he didn't smile I reached out and started to tickle him under his nearest arm pit, until finally he relented.

'Ok, ok, stop, I'm smiling,' he said, and I released his arm triumphantly. We giggled in relief (I did think I might get thumped instead and couldn't believe that the tickling had worked!) The ice was broken. We spent well over an hour with him that day, mostly just listening as all his worries poured out of him. It was the first time he had been given the opportunity to talk about what he had experienced and how he felt about being paralysed for life. His immediate fear concerned sex; he had five wives whom he felt wouldn't be too interested in a husband that couldn't perform intercourse anymore. He believed himself to be unlovable and unacceptable to any woman. It was a practical and a massive worry that I couldn't afford to treat lightly. When he had talked himself out I explained that women were not all about sex and that there were plenty of needs that could be met with communication and respect.

We became good friends and he always smiled the second he saw me in case I attempted to tickle him again. The ward Sister was very impressed that I had won him over and she never gave me any trouble again. A short while later, he returned to Hong Kong and called on his favourite of the five wives. I guess he was a lot more of a gentleman than he used to be and even with his paralysed legs she noticed and appreciated the change in him and took him in, choosing to care for and love him forever more.

His condition was a common one in the ward. There were two guys, either side of him, who were also recently paralysed in shootings; one was a fighter while the other was sunk in a deep, deep depression that I couldn't penetrate. He refused to let the nurse clean him and so he and his bed stank. He was allowing himself to rot away, having completely given up to his injury. Quite understandably, he was angry and bitter and plain disinterested in receiving any help or therapy. It cannot be a coincidence that he died soon after. The 20 other men in the ward were hushed in fear as they watched his body being wrapped up and carried out on a trolley. I was there when it happened and knew I had to do something fast. Depression can be contagious in a hospital room. I cleared my throat and addressed the room.

'Listen guys, yes he has died but only because he practically willed it. You saw it yourselves; he just gave up without a thought for his family and friends.'

Most of them nodded their agreement, and all of them became more determined to keep striving with their physical and emotional therapy.

I visited that ward a lot and got to know all the men. I knew that most, if not all, of them worried about not being able to have sex. I frequently addressed them at large, as it made more sense to have them understand that they basically all had the same worries and fears; 'Being paralysed is not the end of your life. Look at Christopher Reeve.'

Most of them were poorly educated and poorly paid in their jobs, and as a result they attached a lot of importance to their ability to have lots of sex and to doing it well. A few of them started squirming in their beds when I began to discuss loving relationships and the different ways of pleasuring a woman without the penis—this is how I got my reputation for being able to mention Jesus and oral sex in the same sentence. Christopher Reeve, the American actor who had played Superman during the 1980s, had become paralysed after breaking his back in a horse-riding accident. He had recently brought out a video, which had just been translated into Thai, about how his relationship with his wife had actually deepened as a result of his disability. It also mentioned that he could still sexually perform and please his wife. This really impressed the patients and gave them much-needed hope for their future.

I loved working at the hospital, as some of the guys I met there were utterly inspiring. Johnny, from Ubolratchathani, was one of these. Even after losing both his legs and arms he was gorgeous. He had been working on a large machine when he was electrocuted so badly that his four limbs were burnt black and had to be amputated. All he had now were stumps sticking out of his shoulders and hips, yet I never once saw him angry or sad about his misfortune. He was always in good form and welcomed me with a smile any time I visited. One day I told him that I just had to ask if he ever get down about his condition. He laughed and said, 'Of course I get down. I also get scared and wonder how on earth I'm going to survive, but one thing I don't want to do is worry and panic my family any further.'

I asked him what was he going to do when he left the hospital and he replied, 'I have it all worked out in my head. I'm quite good on the harmonica and there is a stand that I can buy which will allow me to play it, and then I'm going to approach a couple of pubs where I know the managers and hopefully one of them will hire me as a musician. I just don't want to have to depend on anyone financially.'

Meeting people like him could only be good for a person.

***

Another project that we got involved in was a drug rehab centre that was set up by the police. Originally it was down to a woman who had donated property—a large chicken shed—and it had been converted into sleeping quarters with unpleasant toilets. It was extremely primitive and by the time Nina and I visited it, it hadn't been cleaned in years. I got some local teenagers to help us scrub the place. People in the area kindly made donations of precious luxuries like tiles and curtains, and cleaning detergents. Some of the teens were tempted to dabble in drugs at the time. Thanks to my history I could spot them a mile away, so Nina and I took full advantage during the cleaning to probe and counsel. It was a satisfying experience on many levels. As in Indonesia there was not much help available for anyone who was hooked on drugs. A lot of them ended up in jail with no chance of improvement as, quite possibly, drugs were even easier to get hold of there. Massive jail sentences were usually handed out to anyone guilty of smuggling or selling drugs and it amazed me the amount of people brave / desperate enough to risk landing behind bars for the rest of their days.

***

My days were becoming fuller and fuller. There was so much work to be done and so many people needed my help. I knew I couldn't help everyone but still I was driven to do the very best I could. Mostly Talya and I lived on personal donations. I worked hard at not panicking if a lot of bills arrived and I had no idea how I was going to pay them. I had to believe that it would all work out. It always happened that just when I thought we were going to end up out on the streets I would, to distract myself from my worries, bring Talya out to visit a nearby slum and give someone our last few baht and then, by the time we returned, an envelope would have been shoved under our door. The donator usually told me how they wanted the money divided; some for my living expenses and some for a project that they had a particular interest in.

I still relied on my 'supernatural voice' to direct me to someone in need of my help. One day Nina and I were walking by a hospital. It was a glorious afternoon and we were chatting away about work when I suddenly found myself interrupting our conversation and telling her that we had to go into the hospital because there was a foreigner who was in desperate need of help. Nina knew better than to ask any questions and we immediately turned and walked into the building. I led the way and headed towards the emergency room. No one stopped us because they thought we were from a foreign embassy. I discovered later that they had called the British embassy and were waiting for its official. We barged right into the room to find, lying in pain and heightened distress, an English guy, Malcolm.

The smell was dreadful; Malcolm was in his prison uniform of considerably dirty shorts and top which allowed us to see his leg. It was huge, rotting away, and there were signs of gangrene; he had blood poisoning all the way to his thigh and the doctors were preparing to amputate. He didn't seem wholly conscious at first—when I think of the pain he must have been in—but when he realised I was talking English he managed to furnish me with a few details. He had been arrested in Songkla for something or other and had been jailed there. Unfortunately his passport had expired and many months had passed before he was eventually brought to the immigration office in Bangkok. His embassy were trying to help him but since he was a little unstable mentally, they were having a difficult time of it. He had nothing to help himself be released or get him back to England. He was stuck in limbo and now he was about to lose his leg.

The doctor was approaching and Malcolm grabbed my hand and whimpered not to let them take his leg.

I assured him that Nina and I would do our very best by him. I turned to face the doctor who told me sternly that he would be performing the amputation immediately. I nodded respectfully and begged the doctor for a respite of 24 hours. I asked if they could try dosing Malcolm with large amounts of antibiotics and vitamin C, and put him on a high nutrition programme, and just see if that made any difference. Malcolm was crying and kept saying, 'Please, please, please.'

Thankfully the doctor was a reasonable man and he agreed to the treatment. We sat awhile with Malcolm until he was calm enough to sleep. The next day we returned to find that his leg had noticeably decreased in size and was looking mightily better.

The day I met Treasure was a good day for me. He was a male Thai ex-nurse in his 40s and I met him at the chicken shed rehab centre. He stood by himself and watched me silently as I chatted with the other inmates. He was in bad shape, having spent the last 15 years of his life as an out-and-out heroin addict. Most of his teeth were gone and he was horribly emaciated, with dark circles around his eyes. When we finally got talking he told me how he used to steal prescription drugs from the hospital he worked at, in order to deal with stress and exhaustion, and after a few weeks of this he became a full-blown addict. He couldn't function without the drugs and, inevitably, it cost him a job that he loved. He told me that he was struck by my honest and open approach to the other addicts. I was even more up-front with him because he was a nurse.

I told him, 'Look mate, you know more than anyone else what damage you are doing to yourself so it's ridiculous for me to tell you what to do. You already know the truth.'

Those simple words reached him and, I'm proud to say, helped him to become clean for the rest of his life.

I nicknamed him 'Treasure' because to me he was a little gem that had been dug out of the dirty, dung heap of addiction that had been his life. He watched his girlfriend haemorrhage their baby down a toilet and had been badly affected by this. By the time I met him he had spent three years behind bars at Klong Prem prison and looked severely ill. We became good friends and he started to help me with my various projects.

***

I was putting together a big anti-drugs programme, with General Sarang, the deputy chief of police, which was going to involve politicians and young celebrities. We wanted to raise the issue in parliament and were inviting top ministers, university professors and celebrities to help us achieve as much attention as possible. Sarang called a big meeting to discuss what we had to do and I went along with a Thai friend.

The meeting dragged on for hours; everyone present seemed anxious to speak for as long as they could, which was fine, I suppose, except for the huge fact that it was obvious not one of them had either seen or taken any drugs, or had had a conversation with an actual addict, ever. They could have all the theories in the world but there was no way an addict or rebellious teenager, bent on experimenting, would give them the time of day. I stifled a yawn. Just as the afternoon was coming to an end, the General called out to me.

'Khun Susan, you haven't said a word. It's your turn now before we finish.'

Now I had to be careful. If you want to impress Thais and get somewhere with them you have to remain polite and friendly, so I resisted the urge to shout out my impatience with everyone in the room and instead begin by paying tribute:

'What an honour it is for me to be among these dignified people that are so concerned for Thailand's youth. I really appreciate being allowed to be present even though I'm a foreigner.'

So far, so good. 'However, I do have one problem with this meeting—we have not once spoken about an actual person. No one has met with an addict.'

I got carried away then and my eyes welled up with tears; my colleagues were shocked, crying, or showing emotion in public, is a very 'un-Thai' thing to do. I couldn't stop the flow of my tears so I just kept talking. All my previous dealings with addicts had filled me with genuine compassion and concern for their welfare; this was a very personal subject for me.

'We need to get these drug addicts on a stage and let them talk about their own lives and experience with drugs. We need to make heroes out of the reformed addicts. They have fought almost impossibly huge battles to wean themselves and their bodies off drugs. They are the only ones who are truly qualified to warn young people about the unimagined perils, financially, emotionally and physically, that accompany addiction. And, by the way, we need to care about the drug addicts—treating them like criminals is not helping them in any way. This programme has to go further than academic theories.'

There was a stunned silence as I took my seat. One of the professors to my right reached for his handkerchief from his jacket pocket, saying, 'That's the most touching thing that I've ever heard. You're not a Thai and yet it seems clear to me that you care more about my people than I do.'

He blew hard into the hankie while others started to nod and smile at me. The General actually made me repeat every word I said so that it was loud and clear what we had to do. Before the meeting finished the agenda of the programme was changed, making it much more relevant to reality. At the next meeting I brought Treasure along. He was given a seat of honour and addressed the meeting about his own addiction and subsequent battles against it.

That was probably one of the high points of Treasure's life but he was not allowed to enjoy it for too long. His story, and our friendship, was to take a tragic twist. One day he was nursing a guy, a former fellow addict, who was infected with the HIV virus. Treasure was trying to re-insert a drip into the guy's blood stream that would pump glucose into him, which he needed to stay alive. The patient lost his temper and was physically trying to prevent his nurse from attending him, trying instead to wrestle the drip from his hand. It's not exactly clear how it happened but somehow he managed to stab Treasure with the drip—the drip that had previously been inside his infected body.

I felt my stomach hit the ground when Treasure rang me to tell me what happened. Up to then he had been off drugs for a few years and he had got his life back together, with a new job, new-found self-respect and a new girlfriend that he was mad about. A certain amount of time had to elapse before he could be tested for HIV and as soon as he was ready I went with him to a private hospital where they would be able to test him and give him the result on the same day. If he had gone to a public hospital he would've had to wait an obscene amount of time thanks to red tape and bureaucracy—my two pet hates. Nobody else knew about it, and I was glad that he let me be with him.

They took a blood sample almost as soon as we arrived and then we were free to settle into the plush surroundings of the reception area, which resembled a 5-star hotel. After a couple of hours I went to the desk to ask if the results were back yet. The two women on reception wouldn't look me in the eye and hurriedly told me that the results weren't in yet but it wouldn't be much longer. I returned to Treasure who was trying hard to conceal his fears from me. After another hour of tiring chit-chat to fill in time I approached the desk again and asked about the results. Again they wouldn't look at me. In fact, this time I would go as far as to say that they both looked very nervous as they replied, 'No, not yet.'

Something was wrong and they were hiding it from me. Treasure must have guessed by my face that something was up and he nervously appeared at my side. The two women tried hard to look over us, left of us and right of us, but never right at us. It was incredibly frustrating and I was starting to get upset so one of them shrugged and began, 'We have found some abnormality.'

This was the Thai way of preparing you for bad news. They started off with something small and ambiguous so that you could brace yourself for the damning actuality. I lost whatever little patience I had left by this stage.

'Oh come on! He's HIV positive, isn't he? You know he is but you're just not telling me. Look me in the eye and tell me that he isn't.'

Again they resisted putting us out of our misery even though it was wholly obvious now what the situation was to all of us standing at that counter. Treasure glanced at me and I could feel myself wanting to cry. He looked resigned to his fate while I desperately tried to keep some semblance of hope alive between the two of us.

'No news is good new, right?' he smiled shakily in reply.

I found out later that the women were trying to locate a doctor and counsellor to tell us that, yes, Treasure was now carrying the HIV virus. They were afraid that if they told him he might take the news badly and try to kill himself there and then in their posh hospital. Therefore, their only concern was for the hospital's good name and not for a man who was waiting to find out if his life, as he knew it, was over. It was night-time when we gave up for that day and wearily left the hospital.

It was to take a mind-numbing couple of days before someone was available to confirm the news, which was absolutely criminal as far as I was concerned. I took the news, which had taken so long in coming, very badly; he was one of my best friends and I relied on him a lot. He was an excellent nurse and had a great way with people, especially children. However, my feelings for him were seriously challenged a short while later when I heard that he had married his girlfriend without telling her he was HIV positive.

My head was in a spin over what to do. I felt it wasn't my place as Treasure's confidant to divulge his status to her so I did the next best thing and pleaded with him to tell her, threatening that if he didn't tell her I would be morally obliged to do so. At the time I thought I did my best but there was a lingering, niggling doubt that I could've tried harder for the completely innocent woman he married. He promised me he would tell her and I chose to believe that my job was done. Very quickly after that they were gone; they moved south and I never saw either of them again. He did send me a beautiful letter in which there was no indication that he had told her the truth. It troubles me today that I just didn't tell her myself; if it ever happened again I wouldn't waste time wondering if it was my place to tell or not. But I have to recognise that there are some situations in which I cannot help.

CHAPTER FIVE

I imagine that when most people think of Bangkok, somewhere in the first couple of things that jump to mind, in between monks and sex shows, is prison. Being banged up behind bars is never going to be easy, but I'm telling you now you particularly do not want to end up in a Thai prison.

Nina and I were so happy about the hospital visitation programme that we wanted to extend it to other areas where people might be lonely, or in danger, and, therefore, in desperate need of our help. It was a very fortunate thing that I knew the commander of one of the prisons that held a lot of drug addicts, Bumbud Prison, and we approached him with our visitation programme. Once again I was glad to meet a man, in charge, with vision, and he welcomed our proposal and gave us *carte blanche* to do as we wished.

Bumbud used to be one of the most notoriously rough prisons in Thailand, and was the first port of call for people arrested for drug offences. In the good old days new inmates were tied and stretched between two trees or else beaten severely and brutally in front of an audience. Thankfully, it isn't as bad now; the commander was a fair man and had worked to improve conditions in the prison although it was still fiercely over-crowded. He took us on a brief tour of the grounds, and that was nerve-wracking in itself. It was very open plan, with just a low wire fence between us and the prisoners out exercising. I couldn't help noting how easy it would be if someone wanted to attack us. It felt like a very long walk indeed as the watchful eyes of a few thousand prisoners were upon us, right and left of our vulnerable path way.

However, I started to relax as I watched men smile and call out to the commander, who was not in the least bit intimidated by these rough-looking men. He maintained a healthy relationship with the men because he still respected them, inmates or not, and they responded in kind. It was a good lesson for Nina and me—at the end of the day every person on the face of this earth is a human being with basic rights, and most of the time you can make life easy for yourself by treating others as you would like to be treated yourself.

We followed the commander to what he called the 'Heart To Heart' house, which was the rehab centre that he set up in the prison. It was usually frequented by the younger inmates, the addicts, as opposed to the traffickers and sellers. They were more fortunate nowadays as before they would have been thrown in with the general prison population, thus making them easy prey for the drug dealers. It was a really good thing now that they were separated from the other tougher elements and got some sort of rehabilitation, and a much less severe penalty. There was already some sort of group therapy in place and Nina and I wanted to improve it, with weekly visits, and broaden its agenda to include bringing in families for therapy so that there was a good communication between them and their sons. It makes a huge difference to a young addict if the family are brought on board. The shame of it is when young prisoners feel like nobody cares for them anymore; whether they're on drugs or not, or whether they're even alive or not. On the other hand you might have to remind the family that this ill-clad, emaciated prisoner is still the child they brought into the world, or the sibling they used to play football with. Some parents have to fight their disgust at their son being arrested for being a drug addict—it's not easy for them to show up and be instantly supportive.

We worked a lot with these parents and guided them in their ambiguous, yet understandable, reactions to their errant children. The boys were being punished enough in being locked up so there was no need to shower abuse on their heads and remind them how much shame they had brought to the family, or that their mothers cried themselves to sleep every night. If someone took that attitude with me I would want to top myself. Guilt can be a highly dangerous tool and best left in the drawer; from my experience compassion and forgiveness are much more effective in helping someone to heal and reform.

One week I challenged the guys about being really honest with themselves. I told them that they would never win a battle against an addiction with vagueness or ignorance. Nina and I asked them to keep this in mind and write down any deep, dark secrets from the past that they had been harbouring, that might be preventing them from getting on with their present and future. They could change their hand-writing and didn't have to sign their names to it. The pieces of paper would only be read by Nina and me and once we read them we would burn them without divulging one word to a third party. It was a great success, with the inmates confessing serious crimes from murder to more trivial ones, such as swearing at their mother. The innocence behind some of their worries astonished me. One guy asked if there was something wrong with him because he couldn't resist spending time looking at his reflection in the mirror, and did that mean he was terribly self-absorbed?

Some of the secrets revealed made me appreciate their bravery in facing up to it. It can't be easy for a little toughie to write about how he slapped his mother around and now wants her forgiveness. I appreciated their co-operation, seeing in it a commitment to their rehabilitation.

Unfortunately, our good works came to an abrupt end. We visited the inmates every Wednesday, but one week Nina had to see her mother that morning so we asked the commander if we could come on the Thursday instead. It then transpired that, on the Wednesday, at the exact time that Nina and I should have been walking towards 'Heart To Heart', two prisoners jumped over the wire fence to ambush the garbage truck. They threw the poor driver from his vehicle and then took the wheel and drove the truck through the prison wall, wounding and killing other prisoners.

The newspapers were full of the tragic events on Wednesday evening. I shook as I read about it; if two defenceless women had been there they would surely have been taken hostage, or worse, and the prison guards would have had no choice but to come out shooting to kill. It brought home to me that Nina and I were risking a lot with this type of work. I looked across at my daughter at the dinner table and sent a silent prayer of thanks that we had postponed our visit that day. Shortly after, the prison was closed permanently to the public, which ended our programme there.

***

The closing of Bumbud didn't end my connection with inmates; in fact a whole new life was opening up to me with new opportunities and challenges, some personal and some professional. The months, and then years, were trickling by. My daughter was healthy and thriving and I found my work stimulating, if never-ending. Sometimes I did try to resist the direction that I was being taken in but it was always in vain. My work was starting to bring me attention from local and international media. When asked to give interviews I would decline, preferring to remain as anonymous as possible so that I was free from being judged or having the expectations of others put on my shoulders. However, I decided one day to take advantage of the situation presented to me. I spotted a young, well-dressed guy loitering around when I was on one of my visiting programmes. I asked him if he was a reporter. He asked me how on earth I knew; I laughed and replied, 'Just a guess!'

He had a nice way about him and I instantly felt he was genuine and trustworthy, so when he shyly asked if he could have a few words with me I agreed. However, as I looked at him I had an idea for his feature.

He was tall, perhaps 6ft or more, and he had an athletic build, lean and muscular. I told him that I wanted him to accompany me to a slum that I had been planning to visit for a while but had been too nervous to go to it alone as it was a particularly rough spot. I warned him that I didn't know what kind of reception we would receive and had no idea what I was going to do once we reached it, but I was compelled, nonetheless, to make a visit. The slum was below the train tracks of Pra Ram VI Bridge. It was mostly hidden from view behind the gleaming buildings that housed numerous businesses and was surrounded by Bangkok Metropolitan Administration's beautifully manicured gardens. I had recently spotted the place from the bus and the squalor just screamed out at me, in sharp contrast with the nearby business offices.

The inhabitants were a pitiful lot; I had watched a few stumble from their shacks half naked and completely out of their minds on drink or chemicals, and this was at approximately 10am on a beautiful sunny day. My journalist friend seemed delighted with my request, but before we headed out for it I visited a generous woman who ran her own bakery. Typically, I left her shop with all the day-old cakes and buns that I could carry. I couldn't do my job as well as I do if it wasn't for people like her. Laden down with our treats we went on our merry way.

At the entrance point to the slum one had to pass by a shabby hut where the district's garbage collectors hung out. I felt a little nervous when I saw them all out, enjoying the morning sun, in shorts and surrounded by empty, and full, cans of beer. Now this could go either way, but I quickly decided to disarm them with friendliness; there wasn't enough room for us to skulk by and there was absolutely no way I was turning back now. So I put on my best smile and bounded up to the group with my bag of cakes, greeting them in Thai.

'*Sawasdee ka?*' (Hi, how are you?)

The men looked up in considerable surprise at this blonde, female westerner waving pastries at them and addressing them in their own language. However, I passed some unspoken test and they smiled and invited us to join them.

'Sit down and have a beer with us.'

I sat down alright but politely pointed out that it was a bit early in the day for me to have a beer, and that my stomach would never forgive me. They giggled at this and continued on with their drinks. They called for their families to join them and allowed my new friend to take photographs of their kids. I thanked them for this and told them that I wanted to visit their community to see if I could be of any help. I had a feeling that these guys 'controlled' the slum and its people, like a sort-of slum mafia. In other words, if I had these guys' blessing—that is, protection—I would be safe to visit and talk to whoever I wanted to. They graciously told me that I was free to enter and even got to their feet to go in with us.

It was a sad, sad place, with drug addicts sitting listlessly in front of the corrugated-iron boxes they called home. Elsewhere we saw and heard drunkards singing, shouting at the sky and each other; shrivelled up men who had gambled away everything they had; bruised women and children, possibly the wives and offspring of drinkers and lots of feeble elderly people without teeth or much in the way of flesh. It could have been a depressing and oppressing experience except for the fact that when they saw me and the journalist offering cakes there were welcoming smiles and lots of laughter. At one stage the journalist nudged me and said, 'Seriously though, it's so bad here what could you possibly do to change it?'

It was an obvious question, but if I stopped to ask myself that every time I faced a situation like this, there would be no point in me leaving my house. I shrugged for an answer and suggested that we keep moving.

There was a little bridge a few metres away at the edge of this slum and when we crossed over it we found ourselves in a second one, the neighbouring community. This one, however, was clean and organised. We had arrived on a good day as it had been declared a community-clean-up day and the industrious folk were out, in their boots, digging out trenches to drain the garbage and waste. After some further investigation we discovered that this slum even had its own bank, where parents could take out loans for their kids' education or for setting up a family business, interest-free. Everyone had put in what they could afford so that it was invested back into the community. What a world away from the first slum, which was mere metres away. It was really interesting to see what people, no matter what class or social standing, could achieve, once they decided to work together. We located the school, which almost straddled both slums, and met with the abbot who worked with the kids. I told him that I didn't have money or property to offer him, but asked what I could do to help. He was a kindly man who could make a quick decision.

'You could teach the children English?'

'Done!' I replied.

He told me to return on the Monday morning and tell the head teacher that he had sent me.

This was a start of a programme that lasted six months. I taught three classes, one after the other, one day a week. I even recruited two teaching assistants. There were two illegal aliens hiding out in a Bangkok refuge—one was from Africa and the other was from Jamaica—who were given sanctuary by a small Catholic organisation. Both were well-educated, highly intelligent men who were bored to death and had nothing to do except wait for their immigrant status to be approved. Perfect!

This was a very special project for me because although I mightn't actually be changing life in the slums, as the journalist had hinted, I was at least building bridges. The kids were really appreciative of our attention and effort; some of them really blossomed under our tutelage. Instead of fearing foreigners and their foreign languages, they discovered that they could learn about them, thus dispelling their fear and instant hatred. We included the other teachers in our work and used games as a fun teaching tool. The kids hugely enjoyed geography, and seemed anxious to learn about the world outside their slum. That was the most important gift we could give them; the knowledge and inspiration that they didn't have to live here forever—they could break out of the depravity and poverty. The walls of the school were adorned with their class work and inspired the kids to take pride in their work. Some days were trying, when some of the kids would arrive to school with black eyes or bruises inflicted by their drunken parents. I had to face up to the harsh fact that I couldn't fix every thing or save everyone, but I could try to make a small difference using what I had.

I had been right to trust that young journalist. He wrote a balanced article and heeded my plea not to portray me as some sort of saint. His article came out in Australia, which I was especially delighted about, as were my parents. My mother told me that she showed it to all her friends. I suppose this was something which properly identified my work, and my life in Thailand, and made it more real. It also helped on a more practical level in that I received a boost of donations from Australians I had never met, which humbled me and motivated me to carry on. My life could be a struggle at times, when I didn't have enough for myself and my daughter to live on, but the support of so many people made it possible for me to continue.

***

The work that I do is like any other job, with good days and bad. The worst part is the frequent realisation that, as with the bruised children in the slum, there is a limit to what I can do, no matter how much I want to change something or turn back time. I am an emotional person and I tend to react to things straight from my heart.

I opened my newspaper one day to read about the brutal attack and rape of a young girl. She was only 14 years old and had just arrived in Bangkok to look for work. Soon after she got off her bus, as she was trying to find her bearings, she was grabbed at Mo Chit bus terminal, bashed on the head and sexually assaulted. It was just a small article with a tiny photograph of the victim, who was now brain damaged after her ordeal. It was a tiny tragedy, only one incident out of many in that newspaper, but something about it wouldn't let me forget it—maybe because I've a daughter myself. I asked around and discovered where she was hospitalised. All I could afford to bring was a bag of grapes.

I met her with her parents, illiterate peasants who were at a loss for what to do with their now retarded child, a former top student with ambition and dreams. They looked haggard with shock and worry as they welcomed me to sit with them on a blanket in the hospital grounds. I offered the girl the grapes and watched her face light up as she bit into the first one. I don't think she had ever had one before. She finished the whole bag while I was there. There was nothing I could do for the family except spend some time with them and show genuine concern for their poor child.

Then there are the times when I'm thwarted from doing something that will make a huge difference. Nina and I were running a weekly visitation programme with the Bangkok Metropolitan Administration Children Daycare Centre. I became smitten with one little five-year-old boy who was thought to be deaf. His mother was a drunkard and addict and it was believed that she had caused him to be deaf with her many slaps to his little head. His name was Dtoon but everyone called him 'Bai', which is Thai for mute. He was a confident boy, despite his background, and loved attention.

One day he slid up to me, when I was playing games with the children, and leant against my body to get my undivided attention. I automatically put my arm around him and spoke into his ear and was astonished when he answered me. It turned out he was deaf in just one ear. I began to teach him English, and how to count and spell. He amazed me with his quick aptitude for seizing hold of and learning new information. I began to envision him changing his life through education; he was very clever and had an excellent memory. I decided that I was going to get him a hearing aid to increase his chances of success and I approached a local health officer who agreed to come to the Centre and test his hearing.

I also received sponsorship to purchase the hearing aid so all I needed now was his mother's permission. She refused to hear me out and, instead of wanting the best for her son, she responded by taking Dtoon away from the Centre. She was afraid that if officials started talking to him they would find out about the abusive treatment he received at the hands of his junkie mother. I never saw him again.

But then there are the times when no matter how little I have, it is enough. A charity organisation once donated 2,000 pairs of shoes, which were sent over from Singapore. I was part of a group working in a refugee camp at the time. Unfortunately, there was a serious management error when it was announced, by loud speaker, to the 10,000 refugees that we were giving away free shoes that day.

It, quite naturally, resulted in a terrible skirmish, requiring armed task force soldiers to try and control the huge crowds that surged forward pleading for the shoes.

It was actually quite frightening and I silently cursed whoever it was that made the ridiculous announcement. The sun was beating down and our task of keeping the crowds in line and trying to match shoes size was growing with the temperature. Women were desperately pushing their young adolescents under our noses and we had to keep reminding them to form a—relatively—orderly line.

After hours of stress it was decided just to throw the shoes, tied in pairs, into the crowd because we reckoned that if someone caught a pair of shoes that didn't fit anyone they knew, they could trade them for food and water. By the end of a chaotic few hours I found myself standing dazed with a single solitary shoe in my hand. The sun was starting to tilt in the sky and the crowd had finally dispersed but for one little old lady who was sitting on the ground; she only had one leg and begged me for the shoe. I walked over to her with this shabby, unattractive, brown, slip-on and handed it to her; she put it on, and it was a perfect fit. As she smiled in sheer delight at me I burst into tears; a Cinderella moment indeed.

***

A riskier undertaking I had already begun was when I started to visit the holding cells in Bangkok's police stations. There were all manner of people to be found in these cells where they were placed immediately following their arrest. I was regularly called down to stations when they arrested foreigners or illegal aliens and needed a translator, so the next step was to meet with anyone else they were holding. I obtained permission from the top guys but still had to ask the head of each station if I could go in. In response to my smile and request, they would grant a rather grudging permission, knowing that I had already spoken to their chief but suspicious that I only intended to report any mishandling of the inmates by their staff. When I reassured them that I only wanted to help them, as well as their charges, they shrugged and asked me if I really thought I could make a difference or would even be listened to by the inmates. I just kept repeating my usual, and only, line of defence: 'Well, I don't know but I have to try.'

And so, after some sweet smiling on my part, they would give in and I would be escorted down to the cells by a couple of guards who would slowly lock the door behind me, as if expecting me to change my mind once I laid eyes on the arrested criminals.

My sudden entrance usually raised a few eyebrows, especially when I started to talk Thai and ask the guys what they had been arrested for. Some had murdered, some had raped, some sold drugs and some were junkies. They usually asked me what I had done to be arrested and found it difficult to believe me when I proclaimed my innocence, telling them that I had come to visit them voluntarily to see if I could help them in any way. The cells were dirty and extremely smelly so they had trouble believing that anyone would want to visit them. Each station had a few cells that were only meant for two or three men but usually held double that or more, and at times I have seen up to 30 or more men crammed in together.

One time I look back on with mixed emotions was when Niall, a mutual Thai woman friend and myself were heading home after a party. As we passed by Muggasan Police Station we decided to make a spontaneous visit. Niall had his guitar with him and we were all dressed up; Niall was in a suit, our friend was in a beautiful silk dress and I was wearing my pearls, so the guys must have thought we were putting on a concert for them. I knew the guard at the desk and he led us down to the cells. We had a wonderful time; Niall could sing many Thai ballads that brought tears to the eyes of these grateful men. He told me afterwards that he had been a little frightened at first because it struck him how vulnerable we were and how easy we could have been taken hostage— something that hadn't really occurred to me before.

The situation took a frightening turn when we finished our visit and called out to be released from the cell. The staff that I knew had finished for the night and I didn't know any of the night guards—and they didn't know me. Therefore, when I rattled the door and informed the guard outside that he could open up now because we wanted to go home, he just laughed and said, 'Ha! That's what everyone says,' and went back to whatever he was doing. It was an eerie moment and we truly understood what it was like to be locked up and ignored. My voice sounded shrill when I called out again, only to hear the reply:

'No way am I letting you out. Now settle down in there.'

I felt myself go cold as I realised that we could be left there, at least until the day shift started in another eight hours or so.

Thankfully, fear led to anger and I shouted with as much authority as I could muster; 'You come here right now! And bring your phone with you so I can talk to your boss. Right now!'

That got his attention. He handed his phone to me through the bars and I rang the General who burst out laughing when I told him where I was. Within seconds we were released. I was drenched with sweat and trying to smile as the guards in the station roared with laughter, thinking it was the most hilarious thing they had ever seen. The three of us would-be inmates needed a stiff drink but, unfortunately, we couldn't afford even one between us.

***

I have always believed in maintaining good relationships with the police and officials that my work has brought me into contact with, and some of them I would count as friends, including the Police General who set up the Village Scout programme on behalf of His Majesty the King. This was like a Home Guard Force that set up to train men how to protect their villages, especially from the threat of communism. In fact, this Village Scout Movement was the largest right-wing organisation in Thai history; it was founded by the Border Patrol Police in 1971 and was dedicated to instilling loyalty to nation, religion and King. I was honoured one day when he told me that he was sending me to be trained up as a scout—me, an outsider! It was a real privilege to be allowed to attend the camp and I set off, enthusiastically, with a Thai friend.

I was a figure of fun when I arrived and the camp elders took great pleasure in targeting me for 'special' treatment. One guy addressed the camp, intending to make fun of me because he thought I couldn't speak Thai. He nearly fell over when I smartly answered him back. It lasted five long days and we weren't allowed to sleep at all. We had to endure things like being covered with cold water and powder; we jumped out of trees and ran for miles. At night, if anyone looked sleepy a trainer would start clashing cymbals to wake them up again. We rested on stone floors that were as hard and cold as they sound. The men didn't think I would last one day, never mind five, and they confessed to spying on me in anticipation of me breaking down in floods of tears—like Goldie Hawn's character in the American film *Private Benjamin* when she enrols in the army, with her long nails and blonde hair, and then realises it's not for her and wants to go home. They waited in vain, however, for that, and found themselves, instead, congratulating me on my strength and determination at the end of the course. They also told me that I was the one person who got the most out of the training.

They were right, because for me it was a great insight into Thai culture and I learned about the important role played by the Thai Royal Family. We were presented with certificates and medals, which I accepted with pride. I was now a scout, which meant more than that I could be asked to join in exhibitions put on by the police and scouts. I took part in events such as international jamboree or parachuting competitions and I also got to meet several members of the

Royal Family. When there was a Royal visit I was usually chosen to present a bouquet of flowers to the Queen, an extremely gracious and dignified woman. I sure she was struck by the fact that when she meets westerners normally they are usually well-to-do dignitaries, not petite blondes in the uniform of a Thai village scout.

CHAPTER SIX

The Bangkok Hilton is almost as popular a tourist curio site as any of the city's magnificent temples. It was built in the 1930s and is a Maximum Security Prison holding inmates who are serving sentences of more than 25 years. It also holds inmates whose appeals are pending in the Appeal Court and the Supreme Court, as well as the prisoners on Death Row waiting to be executed. Overcrowding in the prison is a huge problem, with the population usually around the 8,000 mark. The prison was originally built to hold considerably less than this. There is a pervading sense of hopelessness inside its wall due to the ridiculously long prison sentences and the infrequent state executions. I had passed by its huge walls several times, never realising the impact the prison and its inhabitants would, one day, make in my life. As the saying goes, 'God works in mysterious ways.'

It all began thanks to my American friend Joanna. Her son was in the US army and someone who knew that his mother was in Bangkok had passed on the name of an American guy who was incarcerated in Bang Kwang, wondering if she

would be so good as to check in on him. She duly made the
visit but was horrified and shocked at the condition of the
place. She approached me that evening and begged me to
accompany her when she made her next visit.

'Please Susan, I need you to keep me sane or I'm going to
end up being bitter and twisted, and consumed by my hatred
of the guards and the staff that work there. You've got to
come, if only to give me a sense of perspective.'

I immediately said no, even though I had experience
visiting inmates at Bumbud. Or perhaps because of that very
fact. After listening to her account of the place I knew that if I
made just one visit I would be hooked and I really didn't have
the time for another such demanding, albeit challenging and
stimulating, project. Apart from the fact that my days were
taken up with my youth and drug rehabilitation work, there
was the fact that I lived two hours away from Bang Kwang
and my visiting would involve a journey by car, bus, boat
and then a walk, while carrying food and whatever else the
inmates might need. I continued to say no for several weeks
but Joanna is a particularly stubborn woman and when she
gets an idea she just can't give up on it—which is one of the
things I love about her. Finally I gave in to her and agreed
to go to the prison which was, quite possibly, no surprise to
either of us. I told her that I would be making only one—or,
at most, two—visits after which I would tell her exactly what
I thought, and that would be that. I don't suppose either of
us believed me, but we both acted like we did.

We made an appointment to meet with the Director-
General of the Department of Corrections after meeting
with the American inmate on that first day. As it turned out,
the Director-General had got talking to a friend of mine
at a function and let it be known that he was looking for a

volunteer to head up projects in the prison. I dressed hyper-conservative for the day, wanting to appear as business-like and missionary-like as possible. I wore a black skirt, grey stockings, pristine white blouse, heels, my pearl necklace, just enough make-up, carried a briefcase and even had my hair up in a bun; the party-lover with tampon ear-rings and see-through clothes would have hated it.

Joanna mirrored my image, and we headed off to the Department of Corrections, which was, at that time, housed in a small, funky old building that looked like something left over from a movie set. The guards also looked like old movie extras with their ancient uniform of faded, too-short pants, ill-fitting, colourless shirts and scruffy shoes.

I was there to discuss possible projects with the Director-General. He was the supreme head of Thai penology—it's always better to start at the top and then work your way down; that way you cannot step on anyone's toes, plus you are also perceived to be thoroughly upfront in motive and intent, which is a necessary requirement for my line of business. In turn he introduced us to many other officials. Some of these had never set foot inside the prison and had lots of questions for us. They wanted to know what life was like inside, which was ironic considering they should have known much more than foreigners like Joanna and I.

Our timing was good and that first visit brought me many opportunities and projects. It was as if Bang Kwang had just been sitting there, waiting for me to arrive at its doors. The Director-General asked me to teach English to the penal officers, on account of the large number of foreign prisoners they encountered. The course was duly advertised and quite a lot of officers turned up. Now, this was a good way to make an inroad into the hub of prison life. Thais always look up to teachers, and by meeting the staff in this manner I could befriend officers and administration staff—therefore, people who could help me on the inside.

As they got to know me they started to trust me, which was pure gold, where my ambitions were concerned. Not that I was naïve to think that the trust was solid and automatic; typically there was the concern that I only wanted to expose any harsh treatment of prisoners or bad seeds within the policing and justice system. I had to be careful at all times; I wasn't Joan of Arc, wanting to do battle in broad daylight; my ambitions were trivial in comparison and would need the co-operation of staff, the little guys as well as the top officials.

I met the Commander, or Chief Warden of Bang Kwang—a pleasant and affable guy—who invited me to his home just across the road from the prison. He also hired me to teach his daughter English, and would invite me to functions to do with the prison and penal system. Once people saw me by his side it opened more doors for me. Like it or not, I was becoming a permanent fixture. But I've skipped the beginning of this story: the American inmate in Bang Kwang who Joanna spent so many weeks begging me to visit. In a way, the next part of my life began with him.

**

Garth Todd Hattan was born on 16 August 1962 in Carmel, California, to Mark and Mildred (affectionately known as Honey) Hattan. He was the youngest of five children. His father, a teacher and his mother, a journalist, divorced when he was five, and the kids remained in Carmel with Mildred. Garth enjoyed his childhood with sunny days, surfing, swimming and little league baseball. His siblings, two brothers and two sisters, were very united and protective of their kid brother. When he was 18 he and his mother moved to Long Beach and he attended the California State University in Sacramento, studying music.

After college he became a session drummer, which brought in a decent enough wage, allowing the young musician to develop his newfound tastes for alcohol and marijuana. During a hiatus in his recording career Garth decided to see a little of the world and took a trip to Asia.

He was arrested in Tokyo, for possession of 3kg of amphetamine, and sentenced to prison for seven years. Due to good behaviour, he got out after four years and after a brief stay in the US, he continued with his trip around Asia. He travelled through Hong Kong, Korea, Malaysia, and Sumatra before finally arriving in Thailand. He rented a motorbike to travel around the country. Unfortunately, the bike went up in flames, along with his bag containing his money, plane tickets and passport. Stuck for something better to do, he wandered down on foot to Pattaya beach where he got chatting to a local guy, Pornchai, telling him of his latest misfortunes. Pornchai brightened up as he told him how he could make a lot of money and a free plane ticket to Denmark.

It was simple—all he had to do was pick up a bag in Bangkok and bring it to Denmark. The two shook hands. Pornchai provided him with a suit, to smarten him up, and the bag, which led to his subsequent arrest at the airport by two Royal Thai Custom Officers, at 10pm on 16 July 1994. The two officers afterwards claimed that they had received information from a 'spy' regarding an American male who was scheduled to travel on Scandinavian Airlines flight

HK 972. They had stationed themselves near the check-in desk and spotted a nervous-looking Garth holding his bag of precious cargo. They immediately approached him and identified themselves, asking him to accompany them to their office.

They found 24 tubes of heroin in the bag; the initial weight of the catch was 8.367kg including packaging. After the find was tested for purity, the total weight was 6.173kg. It was duly noted that Garth was extremely co-operative the whole time and didn't, in any way, prevent the officers from carrying out their investigation.

He told them everything he knew and was polite and respectful at all times, which, ultimately, saved his life. Instead of receiving the death sentence, which was usual, under the Thai 1979 Narcotics Act, when caught with this amount of drugs, he was handed down life imprisonment from the Criminal Court on 11 November 1994. On 15 November he was transferred from the Central Correctional Institute for drug addicts at Klong Prem prison to Bang Kwang.

His case was then put before the Court of Appeals where, on 2 May 1995, he received the same verdict of life imprisonment. Garth did not make a further appeal to the Supreme (*Dika*) Court. His case was finalised on 26 June 1995. There was no limit put on his sentence—no release date—and 17 July 1994, the day after his arrest, was proclaimed to be his first day of imprisonment.

On 9 July 1996, the King of Thailand announced an amnesty for all prisoners, whereby some were released and others saw a reduction in their sentences. Garth's sentence of life imprisonment was reduced to 40 years and his release date was set for 17 July 2034, just in time to celebrate his 72nd birthday.

***

My immediate impressions of Bang Kwang prison were of a dark, dour place where the staff looked as desperate as the inmates. From the outside the whiteness of its walls and its seven storey security tower seemed to glisten and dance in the sun, but inside was a completely different story. Although I could understand Joanna's natural inclination to despise the men in uniform who patrolled the place and enforced its rules, I felt myself full of pity for them. To put it bluntly, their place of employment was a horrible one and they were hated by all 8,000 inmates and their families and any other visitors. Their job was a thankless one and they got paid very little for it. No one smiled at all, which made me shudder.

I was used to befriending medical staff in hospitals, policemen in stations, officials in their offices, and even if some of those I met weren't very friendly, at first, there was always one person who would meet me half-way. These men, however, were probably more stressed by their job than anyone else I had met in Thailand to date; they were seriously understaffed and underpaid.

One man who did stand out from the very beginning for me was the gracious Chavoret Jaruboon, the state executioner—but don't let that put you off him. He walked by me one day, carrying a sheaf of papers and his brow furrowed behind his thick reading glasses. I knew who he was because he had been pointed out to me in reverential whispers. I wondered what he was like and how he could do what he did. I also knew that he loved to practice his English, so I called out to him and introduced myself. He answered immediately and we fell into easy conversation. He became my friend and biggest advocate within the prison and was to work with me on several projects. I depend on him today to help me fill out the tiresome paperwork that must be in place before I can gain permission to initiate a project.

He is one of the most honest and practical people I know and always tries to be fair and respectable to his charges. I did give him a hard time when he first told me that he had executed people. I asked him who they were and he couldn't answer the question. It was probably easier for him if he didn't think of them as real people, but I wasn't about to let him off the hook. The next time he performed an execution he was able to tell me all about the person and how they had ended up in Bang Kwang. I think it helped him a lot to talk about the executions and he could trust me not to judge him or exploit his candidness. He is very open about his job in his memoirs, entitled *The Last Executioner*; so called because he was the last guy to execute criminals by shooting them. Lethal injection was brought into Bang Kwang in 2004, finally giving Chavoret the opportunity to resign from his position as executioner, with my persistent encouragement and nagging to do so ringing in his ears.

***

After we were body-searched for weapons and drugs I followed Joanna into the visiting room. This is quite a big room with a wall of wire mesh that separates you from the inmate. Therefore, if you are making a visit on a busy day you will have to shout to be heard by the prisoner you are visiting. While I was waiting for Garth to be brought out I was busy making notes in my head about what Joanna and I could do. My first concern, that day, was actually for the staff and about how I could improve their lot. Lost in my thoughts and making plans, I was slightly bewildered when Joanna hissed at me out of the side of her mouth, 'He's cute, isn't he?'

It took me a few seconds to realise that our guy was being led to his seat. I assume she was referring to his long, flowing brown hair, his athletic, well-toned 6ft build, green eyes and evenly tanned skin.

'Nah,' I whispered back, 'not my type.'

She arched one eye-brow at me in reply. I shrugged ambiguously. Well it was mostly true; he looked like he knew he was good-looking and I, as a rule, don't like men who are into body-building and, therefore, into themselves. Little did I know that we would end up having a relationship. Joanna introduced us and I quizzed him a bit about his life inside Bang Kwang. He asked me about myself, and I, unintentionally, found myself telling him about my wild youth in Melbourne. Only afterwards did I realise that I had wanted him to know that I wasn't just a 'do-gooder' missionary; I was a woman with a past and had, once, been capable of ingesting drugs and alcohol just like him, and hung out with musicians just like him and loved travelling through Asia just like him. And so forth. He had both cockiness and a world-weariness about him that pushed my buttons and I wanted him to recognise me as an equal.

After that first visit Joanna told me that she had to leave for Malaysia and asked if I could continue to keep an eye on Garth. I promised to do my best to visit him whenever I could. She assured me it would only be for a couple of weeks, but then she ran into difficulties in Malaysia when she lost her passport and ended up being away for almost six weeks. I visited Garth every week and also began to target

the jail in earnest to see what I c
returned I had some projects in pl
both secretly expected, I was complete
life and the inmates and staff.

It wasn't easy or pleasant work and in t
place had me frequently in tears. I had quite
own self-confidence as I realised the hugeness
and the hugeness of its problems. Firstly, as
there were the prison guards themselves. Their w
paltry and meant that they were confined to livin
accommodation provided by the jail. Their tiny homes
usually located in the tough, dingy and dangerous distr
within walking distance of Bang Kwang, teeming wi
junkies and gangster-like teens. I visited one home during
the wet season and I couldn't believe how awful it was. The
guard and his family had to lift the TV and shabby furniture
off the floor because of the amount of water around, plus
there was a problem with the sewage system so the water
was not only filthy and smelly but full of dead rats.

The inmates at Bang Kwang could not have guessed at
the abject state of the guards' dwellings. The only guy I knew
who refused to do this was Chavoret; as soon as he could
scrape some money together he moved his young family to
a safer part of the city. In his memoirs he relates how he
had to supplement his wages by playing music at weddings
and parties at the weekend. Some of the other guards that
I met told me about losing babies because they couldn't
afford the proper medical treatment required; others were
struggling to look after sick children and to keep food on the
table. These men seemed grounded down in the depression
of their home life and the depression of their work life. It is
no wonder to me that so many of them are open to bribery

s in the outside
tack in the job
ey were mere

on—from
nt killers
rished,
t up,

ALDOUS

ould do. By the time she
ce and, just as we had
ly caught up in prison
he earlier days the
e battle with my
of the prison
I have said,
ges were
in the
were
cts,
h

way of
ave to believe
stale and desperate
. It is quite simply grim. I
g is a place where a criminal can
ss you consider it such a hell-hole that
be prepared to ever risk ending up in it again,
because you have seen the light and want to live a
ood life to atone for past mistakes. That's fine, I suppose,
as long as you aren't an addict. The fact is, however, that the
sentences are so long that not many people make it back
out again, except for those who know someone important
or who come from a country that has a functioning treaty in
place. Some of those who have murdered are paid hit men
and can usually rely on their bosses or gang members getting
them back out at some stage. The really sad thing is that
people like junkies and paedophiles get absolutely no help
to deal with their demons, and if they are fortunate enough
to be released, after 30 years or so, they can only continue in
pursuing their (un)natural inclinations and might well end
up, before too long, back behind bars again.

The western inmates are generally articulate and
intelligent and they read any legal literature they can get

their hands on in order to build their cases or appeals for transfer to their own countries. Some of the Thais are highly educated and are aware of their rights. It's the lower class, lowly educated guys that I worry about. Some of these are orphaned or crippled with sickness or old age and nobody seems to care about them. Society has apparently forgotten them and they have nobody to fight for their basic rights, and nothing to look forward to. You would be surprised at how many didn't realise they were breaking the law when they were arrested, or how many of them maintain their innocence. It's heart-breaking. You wouldn't treat animals as badly as some of the men have been treated. Prisoners, no matter what they have done, deserve to be treated as well as anyone else. They are human beings who have made mistakes and need help; it is wrong for society to forget them and ignore them, discounting them as if they have been dead for years. Even my good friend Chavoret wonders at the time spent teaching inmates a trade in the prison workshops— what's the point if, on your release, no one wants to hire you because of where you spent your last few years? It says a lot about a society; how it treats the poorest of the poor and the weakest of the weak.

***

One of the first projects that I set up in Bang Kwang with Chavoret involved the elderly inmates. These were the men who had survived many decades of imprisonment, and, therefore, decades of insufficient and un-nourishing food, insufficient or no medical care at all, and decades of violence, either at the hands of the prison guards or other inmates. These are the men that tend to be the forgotten ones, with few visitors and even fewer letters. They try to stay out of trouble and walk about with their bowed heads, fearful of attracting attention; but they got mine. After their years behind bars they are vulnerable to sickness and depression, and when I looked at them I often got the feeling that most of them were just waiting to die. One of the first things to go is their eyesight. Something needed to be done. Around this time I received a substantial sum of money from a kindly, well-to-do Australian woman who was living in Holland. She sent me the money and told me to use it as I saw fit. An idea had been formulating in my head for a while, and this money arrived in perfect time for me to put my plan into action.

With Chavoret's help, I organised for a team of optometrists with eye-testing machines to come into the prison. I helped them to set up in a room that was made available to us. Then the elderly inmates lined up outside, quietly but expectantly. They were all individually tested and then prescribed with the required lenses, which were made up later in the shop. The opticians said that their eyes were far worse than they should have been. Some of the prisoners had lost the sight in one eye and others had developed cataracts and other growths which obscured their vision. We had the glasses made up for less than $16 a pair and one of the happiest days of my life was when Chavoret and I were able to hand these men their glasses. Most of the recipients were aged between 58 and 82 and they were so docile and obedient that they literally held their glasses aloft in trembling hands, waiting to be given permission to put them on.

The room quickly filled with their laughter when they did put on their glasses; some of them were seeing the faces

Above and Right: My parents, Doug and Judy, told me I was the perfect child, with a big toothy grin and blonde hair, happy to sit and gurgle all day. They had no idea what they were letting themselves in for. Thankfully there is no photographic evidence of my wilder teenage years.

Above: With 2,000 pairs of shoes at Khoa-I-Dang Refugee Camp at the Thai/Cambodian border in 1986. I had only just arrived in Thailand and was eager to help in any way I could.

Right: Presenting a garland to H.M. the Queen of Thailand. The Thai people love and revere their hard working Royal Family and it is a great honour to meet them.

Left: Community Police Training at the National Police Cadet Academy. I have always tried, in every way, to become a part of the community in which I am living, and this opens many doors to help me in my work.

Above: I often went to police station holding cells, where I would be locked in amongst up to 30 men, so that I could offer any assistance I could to those who had nobody else to turn to, or just needed a comforting ear. It was always a wonderful opportunity to share some floor space and a word of hope and cheer.

Above: The Bang Kwang Prison visiting area. Until a few years ago, visitors and inmates were separated by four and a half feet, two sets of bars, and double wire mesh. After two hours of shouting and straining in turn to hear over other visitors, I would come away exhausted and frustrated, but all the more determined to make a difference.

Left: Through kind donations of thousands of pairs of glasses from the Australian public, Debbie Singh and Optometry Aid Overseas, the *Eye Can See Clearly* programme helped give elderly inmates at Bang Kwang badly needed prescription glasses.

Right: We were graciously given use of facilities at Bang Kwang, and after raising funds through sheer perseverance, I spent countless hours helping to fit eyewear, make up prescriptions, and offer encouragement to the elderly inmates. It was thrilling to be able to restore simple luxuries such as being able to read and write letters to loved ones once more.

Above: Dear friends and fellow volunteers at Klong Prem prison hospital who hailed from as far as Denmark, Norway and the UK but came to Thailand to make a difference. We helped bring some cheer to the female inmates when they needed it most.

Above: Time out with the ladies at Klong Prem hospital. Many of these inmates were also later fitted with glasses. On this day, a guard sneaked over to me and placed some money in my hand, whispering, 'Keep up the good work.' I was moved to tears.

Above: Mr Chavoret Jaruboon, Thailand's last executioner by machine gun, and my close friend and confidant. Over the years, through his advice and assistance, I have been able to accomplish many of my care-giving projects as he helped me gain access to the prison and outlined the neediest groups of inmates.
© *Karl Malakunas*

Left: Garth Todd Hattan, an inmate at Bang Kwang who would later become my husband. I remember not being overly impressed when I first saw him, but over time we grew to love each other. After visiting him I would have to go for rigorous walks and scrub my house from top to bottom to work through the frustrations I felt at our not even being able to touch. With several other American inmates he was finally transferred to prison in the United States, where I moved with my daughter Talya to be with him.

© Earl Jay Kolb

Above: Humble beginnings in America. Garth and I lived in our new home for eight months; an old VW camper van, crammed full of dreams.

© Derek Dean

Above: Garth and I at our wedding on the beach at Bird Rock, Monterey, California, 24 November 2003. It was supposed to be the first day of the rest of our lives together, but it didn't work out.

Right: Single again after the painful breakup from Garth and a near-death experience caused by illness. I refused to give in to despair and found great comfort in newfound friends.

© Larry Randolph

Above: On my return to Thailand I began to work with a women's shelter where young and first time mothers are always hungry for hugs and personal attention.

Left: My friend Nina and I performing our 'box skit'—a narrated pantomime based on my life's struggles. It highlights that love is the answer to all of life's problems. Performed on Mother's Day in Thailand, we had most of the women and children, including ourselves, in tears.

Left: Smiles, laughs and tears shared with a young mother at the shelter.

Right: As well as working with inmates at the prisons, and the women at the shelter, I also spend some time visiting programmes such as the 2006 Programme for Thai Orphans, based at the Dek Oon Children's Home.

Below: My many commitments and projects are very important to me but so too is my daughter Talya, my own angel.

of their friends for the first time in years and howled at how much they had aged before realising that they probably looked just as old and weathered, if not more so. I don't think I expected it to be so emotional, but it was. I found myself in tears when one old guy, named Wut, shuffled up to tell me how he had prayed for years that he might have glasses in order to be able to read his Bible again. He was beaming from ear to ear and thanked me for not only giving him back his eye sight but also his faith.

After a while I addressed them to warn those who had needed particularly high prescriptions that they could probably expect to experience nausea and bad headaches for the first couple of days. I also implored them to put their names on their spectacle cases, now that they could see to write their names again. They giggled like children at this. Those glasses meant that they could partake a little in life again, either through reading books and magazines, or writing to family for the first time in years. It was a lesson to me about not taking my good eyesight for granted.

***

It's all about simple acts of kindness that can mean a great deal to those who have little. Other projects in Bang Kwang involved me giving out 53 bags of toiletries and food to the neediest inmates. Another time I was able to give pens, paper, sarongs and pillowcases to 100 inmates. The elderly prisoners were delighted to receive a big home-cooked meal one afternoon, which I helped to serve to the delighted men.

The thing is, I depend on acts of kindness and donations from the likes of that generous woman in Holland. These men have nothing and I just want to be able to give them little luxuries whenever it is possible. You just can't begin to imagine the dreariness and grimness of their existence. They have forgotten what it is like to walk on a beach or have a cup of coffee at a stall, or hold someone they love. They are always so appreciative, especially the Thai prisoners. The foreign prisoners are much more businesslike and do not shy away from asking me to do something for them in the outside world. I write letters for them and translate documents for them, and keep them informed of their rights and their embassies. But maybe the most important thing is that I visit these men and listen to their worries.

Visiting prisoners is my entrance to a different world and I feel very privileged when the men are candid about their lives on the inside and what exactly goes on. Penis mutilation was all the rage not so long ago and it was a badge of honour for me that some of the men felt they could discuss this with me. The important thing is not to judge. I have no idea how I would cope with being stuck behind bars for the rest of my life. When you have a community of only men there is a threat to the individual's masculinity. The fairer sex makes men feel big and strong. Therefore when they are missing, men tend to resort to aggression to impose the stamp of their sex. Of course, for some the presence of the 'ladyboys' is enough to make them feel like real men. These are the effeminate men who dress, look and sound like women and they find themselves to be like trophy wives in Bang Kwang. The men who can't cope with these ladyboys have to find another outlet.

Some choose to educate themselves and they take full advantage of the prison library and also the opportunity to do college courses from the prison as arranged by embassy staff or concerned families. Others discover the artist within and become very creative. Others open up a drug-dealing/prostitution business with help from their contacts outside. Others concentrate on their body, and look to differentiate themselves that way.

Some African and Japanese prisoners show interested parties how to insert a ball of polished glass or stone into the shaft of their penises, which duly causes it to swell up with a permanently huge head. Some go further and cut the head so that it resembles a butterfly. Most of the time the inmates end up in dreadful pain, with their poor infected penises, and have to be rushed to hospital to have the offending object removed. If they are lucky enough to escape infection they can show off their penises as they would a fancy tattoo. Every man wants to be a character and they choose their way to survive with a sense of themselves. For men who have been behind bars for 20 years or more they might well have forgotten who they were on the outside or where they came from. It becomes very important to have 'something' in Bang Kwang, whether it is a nice watch, a thirst for knowledge, or a swollen penis.

I had to be careful when I was giving things to the inmates—I had to be careful that they, and not the guards, were the actual recipients. You can't be naive in this line of business and I, also, have to be sensitive about people's feelings. Therefore, I would pass on donations, infrequently, to guards and officials. It's a question of balance and common sense. When I donate food and stuff to the inmates they have to sign a sheet of paper to say they received it. I know all their handwriting by now and the prison officials are well aware that I know all the recipients personally. One of the more outspoken prison guards actually said to me, 'You're so smart!' And we both knew what he meant.

I can't say aloud that I'm afraid that the guards will take something that's meant for the inmates, and the guards can't say aloud that they are affronted by my lack of trust in them. That's what I mean about being sensitive. I simply explained to the guard that I had to account for every cent that my sponsors sent me, and prove to them that the inmates were benefiting from their money instead of me. He nodded and replied.

'Oh right, I see what you mean. That makes sense alright.'

Whether there was any irony in his words I'll never know.

The Thai justice system is, on the whole, very corrupt. That's not to say that there aren't good police / prison officers and officials who believe that it's the rest of the world at large that is corrupt. Thailand is a land of many contradictions; the people are obsessive about personal hygiene and wearing nice clothes, while some of their streets are full of rubbish and dead dogs, at least in the area where I live. There is an unfair judicial system run by, mostly, highly moral people. The police are corrupt but it's easy to see why—the starting wage for a police officer is a mere $100 a month and the new officer has to use his paltry wage to buy his own gun and motorbike. I don't agree with corrupt police officers or prison guards but I appreciate how their circumstances don't leave them with many alternatives.

Of course, the corruption doesn't stop with the little guys. I frequently act as translator for western prisoners in court and have seen plenty of corrupt lawyers who will promise you the earth, moon and stars, take all your family's money, and do absolutely nothing in exchange for your trust. There are also corrupt judges, although I'm glad to say that they are not all bad. I have met some good judges and have taught them English and worked with them. While I'm aware of all of this I have to remain positive and I choose to see the good in people. I have to. How can I encourage someone to do better and use their role in a more positive way if I don't treat them with respect and kindness? I have no use for anger, or self-righteous indifference. When I'm dealing with paedophiles I know that most of them were abused themselves as children, and I just can't forget that and treat them like rubbish. Their own horrific childhoods certainly don't justify their assaulting a new generation of kids but it does afford us some kind of understanding as to what is wrong with them, and how to go about rehabilitating them.

***

I wasn't always this understanding. I used to get so angry, in the early days, with Thais and their strange ways. Every society on this earth has something about it that you wouldn't agree with. People act in a certain way because we are all prisoners of society. I also had a lot of anger towards the embassies here and was critical of them for not doing more or working faster. In the end I came to see myself as a team member who relied on everyone around me to pull together and do what they could do within their own restrictions.

A further example of the contradictions in Thailand is illustrated by the story of Talya's hamster. I had got her a miniature hamster, which was the size of a ping pong ball. She was delighted with it at first but, perhaps inevitably, I ended up looking after it. Every morning when I approached the cage to feed it, it would run towards me wanting to be picked up and stroked. Then, one awful morning, I found him dangling from the top of the cage, its broken leg caught in the wire. My reaction caught me by surprise; it was as if this awful vision released me to react to all the horrible things I had seen in my job and not batted an eye-lid over. My tears blinded me and I was shaking like a leaf. I couldn't allow it to live in agony and so I determined to have him put down. The problem was how. I thought of taking him to Bang Kwang with the idea of asking some relevant inmate to overdose him with heroin, but realised that no one would want to waste their precious drugs on a rodent. Instead, I headed to the vet's office. The vet refused to help me, saying, 'We are a Buddhist country. We can't kill this animal.'

The previous day five prisoners had been executed at Bang Kwang so this seemed a little ridiculous to me and I told him so in no uncertain terms. He and his staff reacted in typical Thai mode to an outraged white woman—they got rid of me fast.

They organised, and paid, for a taxi to take me to Kasetsart Veterinary School, which is under Royal patronage and is suppose to be the best in the country, which explains the massive queue that met me. There were maybe 600 people waiting, with all manner of animals to be dealt with, from dogs to ducks. I took my ticket—number 614—and found a seat beside an elderly man who looked half asleep. I asked him what number he was. He replied that he was number 300 and had been waiting all day. Screw that! I decided to play the manic *farang* card and bustled up to the receptionist as dramatically as possible and bellowed at her:

'Excuse me but I need someone to kill this hamster right now or I'll kill him myself here in front of everyone.'

The din in the room quickly died and I thought I could hear the timid sniffle of a terrified child. The young receptionist gazed at me in bewilderment as I started to howl, and several of the onlookers looked like they might like to volunteer to put *me* out of my misery. I rushed into the nearest emergency room and tearfully pleaded with the staff to terminate my hamster. Predictably they also told me that they couldn't fulfil my wish because they were Buddhists. I pointed out about the executions of the five criminals and the head vet pointed out, in turn, that this wasn't the prison. I looked at him helplessly and decided to try another tack.

'Please, please, please, I *beg* you. He's in terrible pain. Can you not do something for him?'

The vet smiled and told me that he would do something; he would remove the leg. I was ordered to wait outside while they knocked the little guy out and amputated his useless limb. It was a long 30 minutes until the door of the emergency room opened again. I was handed the tiny thing that now had a plastic cone around its neck to prevent it chewing off the bandaged stump. I didn't know whether to laugh or cry.

Men were shot dead in Bang Kwang prison while other inmates were racked by sickness thanks to an obscene lack of medical treatment, and my tiny, irrelevant hamster had just received the best medical attention in all of Thailand because they couldn't bring themselves to 'put him to sleep'. That for me summed up the contradiction that is Thailand.

CHAPTER SEVEN

All in all I didn't do a great deal to improve the guards' living conditions, or their personal life outside the prison, but what I could do was provide them with training courses, through the institute of learning at the Department of Corrections. I also, with help from sponsors, provided them with small luxuries like radios and fans in their offices, and even a new TV in the waiting room. I wanted them to know that I appreciated the job they were doing and any co-operation they could offer me. Some of them shyly asked me to teach English to their kids or translate documents concerning western inmates. I also translated speeches and met with embassy officials, mediating between them and the prison. At that time, my Thai work permit described me as a translator because of the work I performed for the drug rehab centre, and this allowed me to legally work with sensitive papers. But someone didn't like what I was doing, for some reason, and resented the trust placed in me.

That 'someone' made a complaint that I had infringed on prisoners' rights by reading their personal letters, which was completely untrue. Nevertheless, the Australian Embassy had no choice but to investigate the complaint and they called me in for an interview. It was a serious matter. In fact, it was a federal offence and could not be ignored. Fortunately, the embassy staff knew me and trusted me when I explained that the only letters I had ever read were the ones that they sent me. I also told them that this complaint was the result of plain old jealousy and I even supplied the name of the complainer, as it was obvious to me who it was.

I found the whole thing upsetting—it's not that I expect everyone to like me, but I never thought that someone was going to especially stir themselves to cause trouble for me. I could have been arrested so I couldn't afford to take this lightly. I told my interviewers that I only wanted to help people and I had zero interest in breaking the law and risking my projects, and certainly had no interest in exploiting any trust placed in me. I knew and appreciated my sensitive role in the prison and had no wish to jeopardise all I had worked for. The Australian Counsel General listened gravely to me, and was much perturbed that his embassy's time had been wasted by a trouble-maker.

My accuser was a western inmate who had obviously taken a dislike to me and the work I did. He also didn't like Garth or anyone else I was visiting. He was forever claiming his innocence and demanding better treatment over everyone else in Bang Kwang. Previously he had started a rumour that I was a spy for the Department of Corrections and only visited people to find out who was dealing drugs. He was an unpopular guy, who never bathed, and had accused a lot more people than myself—therefore, I couldn't take his accusation too personally, I suppose. Anger at the world seemed to be his motivation to cause trouble for those around him. Even the people who visited him weren't pleasant and I discovered that he had used one of his visitors to lodge the accusation against me, so the only thing to do was give him as wide a berth as possible. Later on, he was moved to Klong Prem where I bumped into him, as I had a temporary office there, scaring the crap out of him. I slapped him heartily on the back and gave him a loud, 'WELL HELLO AGAIN, HOW ARE YOU?'

He paled immediately and looked about him nervously, wondering if I was going to get my own back by having him accused of smuggling drugs. I didn't, however, obviously. It was enough for me to be able to inspire terror in him with my mere presence.

It's all part of prison territory; jealousy, suspicion and rumours. One minute I was working for the government, the next minute the government were checking up on me because they thought I was smuggling drugs. Everyone thinks you're after something. I find it really frustrating because there I am, busting my hump to help people and then I've to make time and effort to fight silly accusations and external influences.

***

Visiting a prisoner in Bang Kwang can be a noisy business with its own set of rules. Generally I maintain good relations with other visitors; they sit in their favourite spots and I sit in mine. Some of these other visitors act like they are afraid I will invade their territory and they are quite possessive about the inmates they visit. Some people definitely dislike what I do and who I visit—I'm only human after all. I'm not exclusive about who I help or talk to; whoever needs to talk, or needs help in any way, I will visit, and I will show them as much kindness as I can. In the line of work that I do I never know when I may need someone's help.

One day I was at the guard's desk in Bang Kwang registering to visit Garth when I found myself surrounded by a group of tall, loud African men. I was visiting very few Africans at the time as they had their own support system amongst each other. Additionally, they had their own church folk visiting them and looking after their needs. I had gotten to know some of their women visitors whose loud booming voices, huge bodies and unbelievably colourful outfits always cheered me up. My favourite was Mama Mafia who seemed to be the one in charge. She loved to wear the tightest black spandex pants and was never seen without her bright, blood-red lipstick. She was a great fan of 'The Lord' and loved nothing better than repeating His words and anecdotes. She also informed anyone who cared to listen that most of her problems were down to a lack of sex.

Back at the desk I was having a problem. One of the men was being overly flirtatious and pushy. By now I had had plenty of experience of these scenarios. I smiled politely and said, 'Excuse me, now I have to be on my way.'

When I tried to leave he grabbed my wrist, saying, 'Hey, I didn't excuse you.'

Crap! This wasn't what normally happened. I thought to myself that if I didn't get away he could follow me. Just then the guard returned to the desk and I was able to pry my hand out of his and walk away. I went back inside the jail and told one of the guards there that I had had a spot of bother. I was a frequent visitor to the prison by now and this kind of behaviour had to be nipped in the bud; I had enough on my plate without worrying about this sort of thing. I hated myself for telling this particular guy because he was known to be heavy-handed with the inmates and had a terrible temper. He wanted me to point out the exact guy but I refused to. I didn't want to be the cause of someone getting hurt. When I finally got to see Garth I told him what had happened and he had the brilliant idea of asking Mama Mafia for help. When Garth's time was up I approached the grand old lady.

'Hey Mama, I got bothered by one of your boys today. Could you tell him to back off please? I'm a one-man-woman and I don't want to be hassled. Is that ok?'

She threw her head back and roared with laughter.

'Oh I love it. A one-man-woman! Don't you worry your head, girl, I'll sort it out.'

She whispered a few words into a colleague's ear and from that moment on those guys were as meek as lambs around me. I never had another problem with an African man after that.

Visiting the prison has certainly resulted in my meeting lots of men which, depending on the men, can lead to its own set of problems. A few years ago I used to visit a western inmate, a junkie who had been in Bang Kwang for 10 years or so by the time I got to know him. He was very insecure about himself and seemed to think that he had to be a certain way in order to attract my friendship. I found it frustrating when he would spout scripture at me, usually misquoting stuff or leaving out the best bits. He would also write to me using letters that he received from missionaries, only he couldn't spell that well even with the original letter in front of him. It was all a front of course. It saddened me that he thought he had to bribe me with spirituality in order for me to spend time with him, but I didn't push him about it. I just wanted him to be himself with me and kept hoping that after a few more visits he might drop his guard and allow us to have a proper conversation.

I visited one day and he was completely off his head. He was so stoned that he walked into the wall, and it then took some minutes for him to locate his seat, sit down and focus on me. I greeted him with a smile and asked him how he was. This time he hadn't got the energy or concentration to quote the Bible, and the truth—his truth—just poured right out instead. He was angry and distraught and his eyes hardened with contempt for me as he spat out his words.

'You want to know how I am? I'll tell you exactly how I am. I saw a poor bastard Thai get beat up so badly here that he was crippled. Right in front of me. Then because he couldn't walk anymore he needed someone to help him. But his mates got tired of helping him so they drowned him in the water sewer. You come here and visit every day but you don't know shit about this place. You've no fucking idea what it's like to be in here. So stop wasting my fucking time by asking me how I am.'

There was a lot more, and I just sat there and listened in silence. Exhaustion stopped him finally, and I was able to speak.

'Thank God, you're being honest with me at long bloody last! I was getting so sick and tired of your bullshit. This morning I thought to myself that if you quoted something at me just one more time I was going to scream until my hair fell out.'

A smile flickered across his face so I continued.

'You're right though. You're absolutely right; I don't really know what it's like to be locked up in this place. Just like you don't know what it's like to give birth to a baby, right? But you can understand that it bloody hurts like nothing on earth and you could empathise with the pain. Talya nearly died when I was in labour with her, and you could try to imagine how horrible and scary that was for me, right?'

He nodded sheepishly and shrugged, 'Ok, point taken.'

We continued on chatting for a while, our friendship starting anew without lies or imaginary walls. When the visit was over the guard, Bulldog, arrived to escort him back to his cell. I had nicknamed this guard Bulldog because he was particularly mean-tempered and liked to throw his weight around with a few slaps, here and there, to show the prisoners he was boss. He was well educated but I think he felt that he hadn't lived up to his father's expectations and this made him bitter and angry; his father was a government official. Quite a few complaints about his violent behaviour had already been filed against him by the foreign inmates and this served to make him even surlier in his attitude. His face was a permanent scowl and he looked like he was capable of growling better than any dog I've ever seen. He also thought of himself as someone who could speak English, and there he couldn't be more wrong. When he believed himself to be communicating fluently in the English language his bewildered listeners just heard a nonsense babble that didn't belong to any particular dialect. I imagine he thought foreign prisoners were being disrespectable to him, when, in reality, they genuinely couldn't follow his orders because they were delivered in gobbledegook.

Anyway, as my prisoner friend followed him back to his cell, Bulldog asked him what I was to him. All the guards knew me because I was practically living in the visitor's room. My friend was feeling happier after his outburst to me so he flippantly replied that I was his wife. Meanwhile I had made the long journey home and was feeling a bit under the weather. It had been a long week and I still had to make the dinner and do some laundry. My forehead felt clammy and there was a distinct tickle in my throat. I decided a cool bath and an early night would be the best. I literally did not have the time to be sick.

Talya and I had just finished our dinner when the phone rang. My friends try to tell me not to answer the phone every time it rings but I just can't bring myself to ignore it, no matter what time of the evening it is. My head was fuzzy with tiredness when I picked up the receiver and said hello. Gobbledegook shot into my hot ear and it took me a while to identify my caller—Bulldog. On top of his usual strangeness he sounded very drunk and I was completely flummoxed as to why he was calling me at home. He continued shouting down the phone for several minutes until he slowly realised that I didn't understand what he was saying. He stopped, took a deep breath, and began to count loudly—one, two, three, four—as if to calm himself down. After several more minutes of madness, while the top of my head was starting to pound with pain, I slowly began to get the point of his hysterical monologue. He had fancied me for some time and had long dreamt of marrying me, but I had betrayed him with my secret marriage to the western junkie.

He felt a fool. How could I have chosen a junkie over such a fine catch as himself? I had let him and myself down.

'Oh Dear Sweet Jesus,' I thought, 'Now what?'

He began to count again, preparing for another onslaught. It was going to be a long night if I didn't do something, and fast.

I sat down on the floor and quickly assembled some threads of logic in my poor pained head, before explaining it to him.

'Would you get a hold of yourself? How could I be married to him? He has been in jail longer than I've been in Thailand. And I think you'd know if any wedding took place in Bang Kwang—it would be all over the newspapers for one thing. Think about it.'

He went quiet and I could almost hear his brain registering my words and, slowly, accepting them to be true. Thankfully I got him off the phone soon after. When I next visited the prison I was very wary of him. I usually like to joke with the guards but I immediately stopped that with Bulldog. His temper and mindset wasn't to be trusted and I didn't want him taking out his frustrations on any of my prisoner friends, especially Garth. A mean prison guard could make life extremely unpleasant for an inmate if he put his mind to it. He could plant drugs on an inmate or even me, so I had to be especially vigilant; I remained polite but distant. I regretted having to worry about him and watch my behaviour, so you can imagine my delight when Bulldog was moved away from having any contact with inmates in Bang Kwang after he hit a couple of British inmates who then, wisely, complained about him to the authorities.

Of course it would be wrong if I gave the impression that it was only the men who caused me trouble. As I said I did indulge in harmless, friendly banter with the guards, which is something that could be perceived as akin to flirtation by Thai standards. However, excluding Bulldog, they all knew I was only joking—and I knew I was only joking—but I forgot about possible third parties. There was one guard in particular who I really got along with. We shared the same sense of humour and he was mad about Talya —though they all were, and spoilt her rotten when she accompanied me to the prison. Anyway, the others would tease him about his *farang* wife; me, and we would take it all in good fun. Things got deadly serious, however, when his mistress got wind of the teasing. For one thing, I didn't even know she existed, and for another, I didn't consider for a minute that anyone would've actually believed we were having an affair since, by this stage, Garth and I were well known in Bang Kwang as a couple.

It turned out that she was the wife of an inmate who was serving a sentence of 20 years and this was how they met, which, I suppose, is sort of romantic, or sort of not. One Sunday evening I decided to bring Talya into town to have a nice dinner. As we walked past the prison that mysterious voice in my head warned me, 'You're going to be attacked. Don't panic and it will be alright.'

I wasn't taking any chances. I put my purse under my arm and turned to Talya, who was about nine at the time.

'Brace yourself honey. Something is going to happen in a minute but don't be scared; we're going to be ok.'

She nodded at me in complete trust. I didn't even have a can of deodorant in my bag but we kept walking. Suddenly, there was a strangled scream. I gripped Talya's hand tightly and looked around. She came at us from the left and held a knife to my face. Her face was red and contorted with her jealous rage as she screamed threats and obscenities at me. I pushed Talya behind me and tried to keep clear of the brandished knife. The woman's over-the-top hysteria made me calm. I slowly took hold of her chin with my hand and, looking straight into her eyes, I quietly and firmly said, 'Listen to me. I am not having an affair with your man. I already have a boyfriend who I love very much. I couldn't cheat on him; it would kill him and me.'

It did the trick and her rage instantly disappeared. She came to her senses and probably, for the first time, noticed the trembling child hiding behind me. She looked mortified and lowered the knife, holding it behind her back.

'Sorry, I'm so sorry. It's just that I thought that ... I'm sorry.'

I patted her on the arm and told her that it was ok—what else could I say? I put my arm around Talya who still looked worried about the hidden knife. Our assailant begged me to follow her to the guard's recreational area where her boyfriend was relaxing. We duly went with her and she bought us food and beer. She sheepishly told him what she had done and that she wanted to make it up to Talya and me for the fright she had given us. She was a different woman now, and looked tired and anxious in the evening light. He regarded her simultaneously with shock and tenderness. I accepted a bottle of beer and toasted both of them:

'Here's to you two. And here's to my boyfriend, Garth, who I love very much—as you now both know.'

After that she turned up at my apartment, still apologising, and now offering to cut my hair for free. Call me a coward, but there was absolutely no way that I was ever going to let her near me with a pair of scissors. No way.

Meanwhile, I was busy with my work, branching out wherever I could be of service, in between bringing up Talya and visiting Garth. My days were full and long, with no end to the problems in sight. It's the impossibly long prison sentences that get me. Sometimes there seems to be no other reason other than that the judge must have been in a very bad mood, so he gives a guy 50 years one day. The next day he's feeling better so he hands out a sentence of 10 years to a guy for the exact same crime as the previous day. When I was helping out at Klong Prem Hospital the doctors told me that some poor inmate had just received 30 years for getting into a fight when he was drunk and giving someone a thump—30 years! His entire life was blown away in an instant. Later on that same day another inmate received 17 years for committing murder. The medical staff was fascinated by this and a lengthy discussion followed, in search of the judge's logic. Unsurprisingly, no one came up with a logical explanation.

The good thing about my work is that I get to learn quite a bit about the way a country is run. I received quite a lot of court work in my role as translator and was always interested to learn new things. The amount of paperwork required for a court case is a huge stumbling block; every little thing has to be documented several times in print. A prisoner's defence involves a truckload of paperwork. The prosecutor interviews his witnesses, who are usually police officials, and then the defendant's witnesses are presented. The hardest thing for westerners to accept is that the judge never ever addresses the defendant, or anyone else for that matter; they just sit in silence on their high bench. There were three judges in the first criminal court that I attended— one senior and two junior—and they would frequently swap over during the one trial. Therefore the only continuity in a case was your lawyer, the prosecutor and the mound of paperwork.

Sometimes the defendant would arrive first thing to await his turn, only to be told hours and hours later that his hearing had been cancelled for that day. Inmates are shuffled in and out, and spend days listening to other cases. There have been times when I've arrived at the court for one particular case and then I've been assigned to anything else that has been going on that day without any prior warning or knowledge of the cases involved.

It is very wearying, especially for nervous inmates who are hoping to reduce their 'life' sentences. As I've said, the judges don't address the defendant but the defendant is entitled to address the judge; only it's best not to. If you look like you're about to say something you will be quickly hushed up either by your lawyer or prosecutor and told to let the experts do their work. If a frustrated inmate ignores his lawyer and addresses the judge he is risking having his sentence increased for his impudence.

As prison legend would have it, one Thai inmate actually took off his flip-flop and threw it at the judge, who instantly added six years to his already life-long sentence. Since then inmates aren't allowed to wear footwear in court. It's hard for a prisoner to make a decent impression on the judge when he is in chains, barefoot and clad in filthy clothes. Normally defendants are allowed to wear civilian clothes but the prisons don't agree with this practice since it makes it easier for the prisoner to escape into the crowds, or else he can have someone paid up to take his place. Imagine that. Some desperate men will, for an undisclosed sum of money, take a prisoner's place—full-time employment indeed.

I have to say though that I think, generally, the judges are not a bad lot. They carefully comb through the paperwork and then make a decision based on that, regardless of their mood. At least that is what they tell me they do. I don't think there is anything personal in their decisions. Sometimes, though, they might hand out heavy sentences as proof that they are not being bribed by the defendant or anyone else. Also, new judges might want to illustrate that they will not be intimidated by the crooks and their colleagues so they hand out long sentences or the death penalty. In a way, they want to protect themselves from the judgment of others. They are monitored by the Supreme (*Dika*) Court and there are always plenty of promotion opportunities for judges who stick to the letter of the law.

I also think that they are careful where western inmates are concerned and don't subject them to the overly long prison sentences—as in they might receive 30 years instead of 50! They like to show foreigners that they are fair men who nevertheless take the law, and, therefore, law-breaking, seriously. The trick is not to look cocky or disrespectful. When my journalist friends wanted to accompany me to court I always warned them to look as 'un-media like' as possible because if the judge thought that I was bringing in the media to pressure him to give a lenient sentence it would probably result in a much longer one than usual. Fortunately, my friends always complied as they did not want someone to lose their freedom permanently as a result of some news coverage.

I'm always careful in court to do things the 'Thai way' and not step on anyone's toes. The 'Thai way' could be said to work on the premise that it's 'nice to be nice'. However, there's always one. I particularly dislike rudeness and arrogance in a person and, one day in court, I came up against a smart ass prosecutor who was a walking combination of these two unpleasant qualities. They say that the eyes are the windows to the soul and they are absolutely right; the minute this guy and I looked directly into each other's eyes over a crowded court room my stomach flipped and I thought to myself, 'Yuck!'

He hated me on sight because I was there fighting for basic human rights, and I hated him on sight because he just looked evil. He even wore a long, black cloak which swirled around him as he entered the court and made his case in the most flamboyant way possible. Naturally Dracula sprung to my mind as I watched him in action. He swanned around the court like he owned the place. This was quite unusual behaviour because arrogance is not a typical Thai quality. He was almost rude, even to the judges—almost. His line of prosecution went something like this:

'Why doesn't the defendant just confess, he'll meet his death if he doesn't?' and such like. Fortunately I kept calm and polite, and managed to resist the strong urge to kick off my heels, spring over my desk and clock him right in the mouth, exactly like Simon had done to me all those years ago. Afterwards we sniggered like naughty children when one of the other translators showed me a sketch he had done of Mr Evil, which perfectly captured his big nose, scrawny neck, black eyes and ridiculous cloak—a dastardly villain indeed.

CHAPTER EIGHT

Meanwhile Garth and I were getting on just fine; well, except for the fact he was being held in a maximum security prison and was a junkie. He was a challenge to me in the beginning. In fact, for a while I don't think I even liked him much. He was this cool dude who flicked his long hair in people's faces just to annoy them. When I first knew him, pleasure was his number one hobby; in the form of sex, drugs and rock 'n' roll. He had a fancy townhouse and BMW courtesy of the drug trade, and he got stoned every night of the week. Every morning there was a different girl in his bed—especially true in Thailand. He certainly loved it here, until he got caught. Up to then he hadn't a care in the world and just lived completely in the moment. This was certainly illustrated by his spending habits. I almost choked when he told me what he used to spend on drugs, alcohol and prostitutes—I could've fed a small third world country for a week.

It took a while to break through his 'tough guy' exterior, and I suppose I had to prove myself to him too. He wasn't religious in the least and refused to believe that I visited prisoners and gave them gifts merely because I wanted to do something positive for others. I think he was afraid that I'd contaminate him with my spirituality and Miss Goody Two Shoes existence. He had this fear that he would become a community pet project, something which his manly pride couldn't have dealt with. Perhaps you could compare it to the tentative relationship that grew between the stand-offish Captain Von Trapp and the novice nun Maria in the film, *The Sound of Music*. It was a long, long time before he rewarded my patience with his confidence.

As far as I was concerned, early on, I was already too busy and fulfilled by my work. I wasn't looking for a relationship and especially wouldn't have advocated falling for a client, and especially if he was a long-haired, arrogant American with an, 'I'm too cool for you,' attitude.

But you don't choose who you fall in love with and I'm not about to start explaining why or how. It just happened, despite all the warnings I received from Bang Kwang's well-meaning staff. The prison warden called me into his office one day and delivered a stern lecture, which reduced me to tears.

'Listen Susan, you seriously cannot be involved with this man. You have got to be careful, there are so many people here who look up to you and trust you. What will they think about you hanging around this dirtbag?'

I had to keep repeating a mantra in my mind: 'He means well, he means well, he means well,' but it was difficult. I couldn't bring myself to tell Garth about the warden's words. It wouldn't have done either of us any good. There was also a lovely young nurse who worked at the prison. She used to give me donations and little gifts whenever she could. One afternoon she approached me and without looking directly at me she stammered out her words:

'Please Susan, I hate saying this but you're my friend and I care about you. Please don't get involved with Garth, for your own sake.'

She looked very uncomfortable and I knew it had cost her to say what she had to say to me.

The guards certainly made their feelings known. The more aggressive ones would pretend that Garth had been busted and sent on to another prison, just to see me freak out, while others would mumble under their breath, barely audible, 'The guy's a loser,' and would ignore me when I looked at them.

I could never challenge them for fear that I wouldn't be let visit Garth, or he wouldn't be let see me. All I could do was smile politely and say something jokey in return, just keeping it light while my insides churned. There was certainly no love lost between the guards and Garth; he had no respect for any of them and refused to play the role of co-operative prisoner. He hated the fact that I would have a laugh with the guards and it took some explaining on my part to point out that having the guards on my side could only help me and anyone to do with me. Some of the more unpleasant prison guards could be particularly nasty to visiting girlfriends, just to get at an unpopular prisoner. I've heard of some young girls being blackmailed for sex, told that their guy would suffer if they didn't comply. What saved me was that I had good contacts and was a foreigner. I was also good at joking my way out of situations, all the while getting my point across about what I would, or wouldn't, accept.

Garth also didn't have many friends among the prisoners, Thai or foreign. He was an arrogant American and a bit of a loner who found it hard to get on with, and trust, others. This also proved a bit of a sticking point in the early days of our relationship, this lack of trust. Nobody wants to get hurt. When I first started to visit Garth, I was still smarting from my break-up with Niall. Garth wasn't looking to make his life even worse than it was so we both wanted to protect ourselves. All the same, neither of us wanted to put an end to my visits.

He started testing me a little with sexual innuendo. Now remember, he was behind a fence when I went to visit so we couldn't touch one another ... for a few years! He wrote me letters tentatively describing his dreams or fantasies of making love to me on a secluded beach, with the sun tipping towards the horizon and the sound of the lapping waves in our ears. Our conversations became deeper and deeper because they were all we had. We couldn't waste time staring into each other's eyes since we only had one short visit a couple of times a week, plus the visiting room was so insanely noisy that it would've taken a better person than me not to keep talking as loud as I could, to drown the other visitors and prisoners out. And like any other relationship we had our bad days.

Sometimes I would doll myself up to see him, after racing through what needed to be done that day, and charge into Bang Kwang like an excited little girl on Christmas morning, only to find he was in a bad mood and utterly depressed with life behind bars. I tried my best to hide my disappointment, especially since I completely understood what he was upset about. But when it happened a few times in a row, and then he started moaning about what I did, or didn't, write in my letters to him I snapped;

'Hey, I know you're upset and I want to be here for you, but I'm only human. I'm not the enemy—I'm on your side. So could you give me a break ... or a smile, please?'

He did his best but as time went on I noticed he was looking more and more frustrated and I worried that he'd get into a fight with a guard or another inmate or just little old me. I had a feeling about what was going on but I wasn't sure how he'd take my addressing it. Then I just thought to myself, 'The hell with it', and asked him the sixty-six million dollar question:

'When was the last time you jerked off?'

He nearly fell off the chair and stared at me as if I had just let off the most enormous, stinking fart. His face reddened as he stuttered out the fact that he hadn't indulged in that particular sport since arriving in Bang Kwang. I tut-tutted and told him that it was unnatural and unhealthy to abstain, and it was making him angry and aggressive. He didn't look very convinced and I felt I was way, way out on a very small, vulnerable limb. I sent him an article on the benefits of masturbation but I think he still thought I was a lunatic. However, it must have worked because he certainly became a lot less aggressive.

Bit by bit, or visit by visit, we started to draw closer in spite of the physical restrictions. We both opened up about our past and about our families. He felt he had let his down badly and found it difficult to get past his shame and write to them. I asked him to let me help and as a result I built up a good relationship with his mother. She was really appreciative of the fact that I loved her wayward son and didn't judge him for his past doings. She had never given up on him and still saw in Garth the little boy she had raised.

The rest of his family, understandably, found it a bit more difficult as they felt they had been through the mill with him already. They were still too angry to be able to contact him yet. For my part, I waited several years before telling my own family, correctly guessing that they weren't going to be jumping for joy.

I found it so refreshing to be able to talk to someone in English. Also, Garth was a good listener and didn't let me away with being glib or casual. He constantly challenged my philosophy on life and the motives behind what I did. I welcomed his questions and opinions. It was the first time that someone had been this interested in me as a person and not just as someone that would help you learn English or bring you cakes in prison.

I cracked first and said that dangerous four-lettered word, following 10 months of visits. We were having one of our talks and he had absent-mindedly pushed a strand of hair out of his eye; suddenly I was filled with a rush of something and interrupted him with my declaration, 'I'm going to love you like you've never been loved before.'

I think I looked as shocked as he did. We had been skirting around the subject for some time and I was pretty sure of our growing commitment to one another. At one point he panicked, saying, 'Hey, you have to remember I'm in a very vulnerable position. You could meet someone else tomorrow and I'm still locked up here.'

I assured him that I wasn't planning on hurting or deserting him. After a few more visits I became restless with my unacknowledged feelings and, once again, broached the subject.

'Garth I've fallen for you. I love you.'

He exploded in anger at me: 'How can you say that to me? How can you love me when I can't love you? You don't even know me properly.'

I understood, however, that he was angry because he felt he had nothing to offer me—no future to spend with me. The American-Thai transfer treaty stipulated that anyone trafficking over a kilo of Class 1 drugs did not qualify for transfer back to the States. At that time it was much easier for a paedophile or murderer to get out of prison than someone caught with even a small amount of drugs. Some prisoners could take advantage of the treaty which allowed American prisoners to leave Bang Kwang after eight years and return to America to complete their sentence, but not Garth at that time. It would take some time for it to be considered in Thai courts that even if some of these guys were caught with a large amount of heroin, or other drugs, it didn't necessarily mean that they were the masterminds of the operation. This change and the subsequent removal of the clause from the treaty came about due to a woman inmate's appeal. Most of the time, as her case would argue, the ones who were arrested were just the addicts or desperately poor people, and not the kingpins of the drug trade. Those ridiculously long sentences weren't helping anyone—they were just too much, too late.

I'm glad to say that the situation has vastly improved now. Drug addicts are no longer locked away for the rest of their natural lives; they are treated as opposed to merely punished. But there was no light at the end of the long dark tunnel back when I told Garth I loved him.

I used to cry alone in my bed at night imagining what it was like to be locked up for 30 or 40 years in Bang

Kwang. Because of Garth I now had to truly consider what that actually meant to a person. When I thought of the hopelessness that Garth was experiencing I felt an actual pain in my chest. It was such a huge obstacle and there was nothing either of us could do about it. In my line of work I was used to dealing with and overcoming situations that had initially seem impossible but I couldn't work my way around the walls of Bang Kwang and the Thai penal system.

It was a peculiar situation—sometimes I'd be so angry at him for breaking the law and getting himself banged up, but then I'd remember that if he had never been involved with drugs he would never have been arrested and we'd never have met. Time and time again I would dream that he was free to walk down the street holding my hand, free to have dinner with me and Talya in my favourite restaurant, free to help me carry home my groceries, free to kiss me after a soppy movie. Then when I'd wake up, in the bed of the house that Garth had never seen, the bleakness of our future would nearly keep me buried under the duvet, unable to face the day. I'll be honest; I did go through phases when I questioned my sanity—when I couldn't see much point in continuing to visit someone who could never take a walk outside in the sun with me.

I took a walk one day and went for a coffee. The sun was high in the sky and I people-watched for a while. I probably looked quite passive to the other customers but there was a battle raging within.

'I'm going to get hurt, I'm going to get hurt. I should just end it now,' versus, 'I love him; he gets me, I get him. Just have faith that it will all work out in the end.'

I did crawl away in tatters when he said he couldn't love me in return. I shrugged it off for the duration of the visit and then brightly told him, as usual, to take care and I'd see him the following week. I spent the next few days trying to wean myself off Garth as my soul mate and instead tried to focus on Garth as a foreign prisoner in Bang Kwang in need of shower gel and someone to talk to. In reality his needs were a little more serious than my romantic ones. I thought I was getting the hang of it and didn't even put on lipstick when I went to visit him next. I greeted him as I would any of my other incarcerated friends and had a couple of safe topics in my head to enable a good, old-fashioned, platonic conversation. However Garth had been doing some thinking about our previous chat and was delighted to be able to share with me the fact that he loved me too. Oh well!

When I watch old black and white movies from the 1930s and 1940s they always remind me of my long years of chaste visits with Garth—the smouldering desire that could not be gratified on screen because of the censors. Instead, the director would show what he couldn't through the looks that passed between the lovers, as well as their words, and let our imagination finish the story. It was difficult, however, to achieve the perfect smouldering look over 4.5ft, including two sets of bars and two sets of chicken mesh wire fencing; for a long time I wasn't even 100% sure of the colour of his eyes. After a particularly flirtatious visit I would have to power walk for a while, in order to dilute the 'energy' (read 'frustration') that consumed me. Even then, when I'd get home, I'd have to scrub the house on my hands and knees whilst pondering on whether a human being could actually spontaneously combust. It was not easy. I began to spend a worrying amount of time thinking about sex—I figured this had to be what it's like inside an average guy's head.

We didn't even know what the other smelt like, which I think is a huge part of falling for someone. Do you ever shut your eyes to think about someone you loved once, remember hugging them and breathing in their scent? We hit upon the idea of exchanging tee-shirts after sleeping in them; it was the next best thing. I would then sleep in his shirt and he'd sleep on mine and then when our smells wore off we'd make the exchange again for more, like addicts.

After two years the guards let us visit in the room that the embassies' staff used to meet their charges. There was still a mesh and wire barrier separating us but it was a much quieter room. During the first visit in that room we discovered that one part of the mesh was torn, allowing us to touch fingers—I cannot begin to describe what that was like. All I will say is that I don't think either of us slept that night.

I showed my love in wifely ways like cooking him something he liked and bringing it in to him. I also pursued the embassies and helped sort out legalities, or whatever he needed done. And I introduced him to my daughter. As a young kid Talya accompanied me a lot on my prison visits. She was adored by the guards, especially Chavoret, who introduced us to his wife, Tew, and family. Garth fell for her too and they struck up a good friendship. When she struggled with her homework and I couldn't help her she would tuck it in her schoolbag and come with me to the prison where Garth would sort out her maths problems. They wrote long chatty letters to one another and I found it wonderful to have someone as concerned with her welfare as I was. He shared the weighty matter of parenting a young, impressionable and intelligent child.

He became involved in my prison work and would root out hard luck stories and tell me who was particularly deserving of a toiletries gift bag or whatever I could get my hands on. It was gratifying to see him taking a genuine interest in others and want to do something to help them. He befriended another inmate, Aree, and they took great fun in playing 'Secret Santa'; I would give them stuff and they would sneak it into another guy's locker or mattress.

Men always accuse women of trying to change them and there is an element of truth in that. I didn't have much time for a pretentious surfer dude who just wanted to play his drums and get stoned, so yes, I did encourage him to develop his new interests that mirrored mine. Of course, he still managed to mess up from time to time. A particular favourite of mine was when he seemed troubled one day and I, foolishly, asked him what was up, only to be told that he had serious concerns about not finding me attractive on his release! I was so stunned that I couldn't react ... until my next visit, a week later, when I let rip at him for being a superficial fool. I was 35 years old and quite happy to accept that I wasn't Peter Pan, but he had hit a nerve nevertheless.

***

At this time Talya and I were living with Nina in a house, Radboorna, belonging to our friend Surin. He also ran a school where Nina and I taught and kept the house for his teaching staff. My days were filled with prison projects and school work but something was wrong. I had a cyst which I was trying to ignore but it was starting to make itself felt. Then, one bright February morning, I sat down on the toilet and found myself in great difficulty. I doubled-up in shock at the pain that hit me out of the blue. My body broke out in a cold sweat and everything went blurry; there was a clanging noise in my ears like the pain was a separate entity and was shouting at me. I fell off the toilet and onto the floor. I only managed to reach the door handle by clinging onto the side of the bath to support myself as the pain incredibly worsened. I need hospital treatment and fast. I booked into the private hospital where my gynaecologist worked. I had known him for a while and liked him. However, I was distressed to read in his notes that he was going to perform a hysterectomy on me, without actually telling me first.

I put my foot down immediately and refused to let him do it. I told him, instead, to just remove the problem ovary, or as much of it as was truly necessary. I couldn't believe that he wasn't going to ask me about what he wanted to do, and he couldn't believe my reaction. There was further scandal when I informed him that I wanted to remain awake during the operation. He gasped and said that this wasn't standard procedure and that I would surely pass out from the pain. I stood my ground, however, and he had no choice but to agree to it. News spread around the hospital that a *farang* woman was choosing to be conscious throughout her operation. I had a very good reason for wanting to be awake in that I had recently read about some poor guy who woke up after a minor operation to discover that one of his kidneys had been stolen for another transplant operation. I was not taking any chances. I was absolutely terrified but also equally determined to go through with it.

I was hospitalised for five days and had the operation on the first morning, Thursday. Garth was very worried about me and his imprisonment was emphasised when we realised that it would be a while before he would hear how I was and if the operation had been a success. Before my operation I was injected with a large dose of morphine into my spine to help with the pain. However, it wasn't an effective enough quantity because I was so thin; if I had a bit of extra weight on me the fat would push against my spinal column, allowing the morphine to be processed faster into my system. Therefore, unless they wanted to overdose me, they weren't going to be able to give me the required amount to make the operation a painless experience. However, by this stage, they were more worried about the situation than I was, because I was starting to feel mighty fine, and whistled and hummed and maybe even giggled; just soaking up those morphine vibes.

I had asked for a mirror to be installed over the operating table so I could watch the proceedings. The operation would be bloodless, so watching wasn't as traumatic as it might've been. I could smell my burnt skin though as they burnt and cut. I felt like a barbequed chicken. At some point I saw the surgeon pull at something which he introduced to me as being part of my intestine. My insides were like a painting— I never realised that we had so many different colours inside us—everything is colour coded. Probably to keep me calm, the staff started to chat to me as if we were out having dinner together. They were curious about what I did for a living and why I chose that way of life. The anaesthesiologist had remained in the room to monitor me throughout the operation, just in case I needed more morphine. They were fascinated by my chosen career and were even more so when I told them that I had very little money, that in fact I barely had the taxi fare to get myself to the hospital. And now I was to stay in this private hospital for five days. I explained how money always turned up just when I needed it most; that it was all a matter of faith.

Something of what I said really struck them, and I was moved to tears when the surgeon and anaesthesiologist told me there and then that they wouldn't be charging me for the operation. The two hour operation took four hours thanks to our interesting discussion on life and death, how to deal with grieving relatives and how to prepare terminally-ill patients. When they were finished I asked them to knock me out for the sewing up part, as, by then, I completely trusted everyone present.

I woke up sometime later, thankful that it was all over. Not many people had been told about my operation, I knew I wouldn't be up to lots of visitors. So, I had a lot of time to worry about things, from my finances to my life in general. As a result I felt very alone and a little frightened about what the future had in store. Nina was going to come by with Talya, whom I was anxious to see. Also, of course, Garth was on my mind. If I could only pick up the phone and talk to him, I thought, but this was impossible since, at that time, he was being held in Building 10, which was solitary confinement. I had previously come up with the plan to have a request played for him on a popular radio station. He had borrowed another inmate's walkman and was nervously waiting to hear from me.

I rang the station, 95.5, and told the receptionist that I wanted to make a dedication live on air. She asked me why and I explained that my boyfriend was in solitary confinement in prison and that I had just come through an operation and I needed to let him know that I was going to be alright. Within seconds I was greeted by the DJ who asked me my name. I told him that I just wanted Garth to know that the operation went smoothly and I was on the mend. I also wanted to tell Garth that I loved him and he was my hero. The DJ asked me incredulously how an inmate at Bang Kwang could be my hero and I replied without thinking:

'Because he loves me unconditionally; who I am, what I am, and I feel the same way about him.'

'Wow,' said the DJ, 'that's good enough for me. What song do you want to play for him?'

I didn't have to think about that. The Australian band, Savage Garden, had a popular song in the charts at the time and I felt it could have been written with me and Garth in mind. 'I would like you to play "Truly Madly Deeply" please.'

The lyrics perfectly captured all that I wanted for us, all that I wanted to be for him and him for me; my wish, my fantasy, my hope, my love, and it also spoke about the new beginning that we wanted together. It also spoke about standing on mountain tops and bathing in the sea, which, of course, meant freedom to enjoy each other out in the world around us.

This was it; I had just declared my love for a criminal on national radio. Everyone would know now, from my contacts in the top echelons of Thai society to the other inmates in Bang Kwang. There was no turning back. God knows what sort of reactions I was going to get—declaring my love for a drug dealer who was currently in solitary confinement was taking a huge risk in terms of my reputation. The Thais were always so polite and curious. They had also put me on a sort of pedestal and liked looking up to me as something pure and exotic. I was in agony in that hospital bed—it hurt to reach for the phone on my night stand. The morphine wasn't enough to deaden the pain and I was still quite groggy from being knocked out. Nevertheless, I cried my eyes out when I heard my song and the DJ's kind words about real love, when it had finished.

Meanwhile Garth was having an epiphany about our relationship. He had been really scared for me and had been forced to imagine how he would feel if, perhaps, I hadn't survived the operation. He even found himself praying for me. I don't know who would have been more surprised about this outcome; Garth, me or God! Later he told me that he, too, had cried his way through the song. The whole event was directly responsible for pushing our relationship on to the next level; we were now committed to one another, for better or worse. When I next visited the prison a Nigerian inmate congratulated me on the radio stint. He thought it was really romantic and brave. Garth had told his mates in solitary confinement to listen out for me and they all reacted positively to it; a bit of old-fashioned romance goes a long way, even in Bang Kwang prison.

***

I was sharing my hospital room with four other women. One of them had been getting on my already fragile nerves. She was in pain like myself and spent a good part of the night talking to someone on her mobile phone, complaining about her misery and illness. I couldn't see her as the curtain was pulled around her bed but I was scowling in her bed's direction, fretting that her whining was going to prevent me from getting a badly needed good night's sleep. She was upset that nobody had been to visit her and, after a while, I found myself feeling sorry for her. I suppose she was only as lonely as I felt. I never knew who it was she was talking to but I fancied that her loved one also couldn't be with her, and when she finally got off the phone I struck up a conversation with her. We were able to offer a little comfort to one another and when I was let go from the hospital I went back in to check up on her. It hit me that I could be more genuine in my empathy for someone else since I had personally gone through feelings of utter isolation and persisting financial worries. It was something about which I could be glad—the whole experience—the cementing of Garth's feelings for me and that it was another notch on my belt for people to trust me with their problems.

As for my worries about how on earth I was going to pay for my hospital bill; once again I was looked after. The doctor and anaesthesiologist had waived their charge but I still faced general hospital bills. I had prayed and prayed about it, going through my options. There were always my parents, of course. They would never deny me anything, but if I asked them for a loan I'd have to tell them what it was for and I really didn't want to worry them any further than was necessary. Nina had brought in Talya and knew about the situation but she had even less money than I did. I told her not to worry, that it would all work out in the end—probably to convince myself as well as her.

Meanwhile, an old friend of mine had turned up. She was the daughter of a wealthy general I knew, and when she was a troublesome teenager, refusing to go to college amongst other things, he asked me to take her into my home. She ended up living with me for six months and proved to be a hard worker and willing helper in the projects. She also discovered a talent, and liking, for looking after people and had gone on to be a stewardess for Thai Airways. Her parents had told her I was in hospital, and she later told me that, on her return from a flight, she was at the gym when she suddenly heard a voice in her head telling her that I had saved her once, and now it was her turn to help me out. She left immediately for the hospital where I was and secretly paid the bill with money she had put away to buy a car. She visited me later at home and told me that it had been her who had helped me out. I will never forget what she did, and it was further proof for me that when you do good and bad in the world, it always returns to you like a boomerang.

When I got home the house was in a terrible state. Surin, the owner, had decided to renovate so I arrived back, in my weakened state, to a construction site. I know I should've tried my best to ignore the mess and take a few days to recuperate in bed, but that's just not me. I cleaned and scrubbed as best I could, without bursting my stitches. I couldn't actually stand so I had to crawl around, for five hours. It was awful but I wouldn't let myself rest. For one thing, there were cockroaches everywhere, so there was no way I wasn't going to worry about them in the food, or the bins, or in my laundry. I even washed clothes and made the dinner, and seven days later I was back in the prison. I later wrote to my friend, Anne, who was to undergo an operation, and urged her not to follow my insane example, telling her instead that it was important that *she* rested when she came out of hospital.

CHAPTER NINE

G arth was a talented writer and penned articles for a magazine, *Farang*, which was set up for ex-patriots and travellers to Bangkok, from his cell in Building 10. He railed against the long prison sentences for addicts and wondered at how someone could be rehabilitated against taking drugs again, by dumping them in solitary confinement. He wrote these sweet words once:

*

Some of the guys I've been hanging out with here have illustrated that I can feel fortunate because I have the luxury of being the citizen of a country which has a treaty agreement with the Thai government that allows me the opportunity to return home very shortly. Even if it's having served in these dank conditions for eight and a half years. They have a valid point, as most of these guys had been incarcerated many years before I walked through these gates, and many years after I've left they will still be wondering when they shall finally have the opportunity to return home themselves. I don't have any witty, intelligent response to such tragic injustice.

Other than my luck at possessing a US passport, I've been blessed with something throughout the last six and a half years of this crisis which no one else here at Bang Kwang has had. All those years back, a striking Australian woman came to visit me and evidently saw something in me which even I hadn't seen in myself up until the time I had inadvertently altered my personal fate. It had been a rather graphic dichotomy: amid the ugliest period of my life I'd been introduced to the greatest of it as well. I've written about her in past articles, and could write chapters of how our relationship has evolved. What I can't write yet about is our future, which is soon to unfold.

*

What indeed was to be our future? After four years of visits, two of which were granted contact visits by the guards, allowing us to kiss, hold hands and eat together, Garth asked me to marry him on 5 August 2000. He gave me a ring that had belonged to his grandfather and I was proud to wear it. Things had changed legally due to that female inmate's appeal against the one kilo clause in the treaty with America. Initially Garth was supposed to get the death penalty, but because he cooperated fully this sentence was reduced to life imprisonment, and now due to the female prisoner's campaign, he became eligible to return to America after serving eight years in Bangkok.

Things certainly seemed to be looking up for us when we then heard about a mass amnesty on the occasion of the Golden Jubilee. Sometimes, on days of celebration, the Royal Family might decide to reduce the sentences of prisoners, as a gesture of goodwill. Word had it that foreign prisoners with a 'number' sentence, that is convicts with long and definite sentences of, say 30 or 40 years, could return to their own countries after serving just four years, while those serving life imprisonment could return after eight years. This became official news after a while, even to the point where the relatives of inmates were informed of early releases. There was great excitement throughout Bang Kwang as you can imagine, and many tearful phone calls were made home to ecstatic relatives. In the amnesty, Garth was given a number sentence instead of his original life imprisonment, which meant he could be out after serving four years, most of which he had already served by this stage. We couldn't believe it, and started to make plans for a future that was suddenly more real than it had been all along. But, just as suddenly as our hopes were raised, they were suddenly dashed to the ground once more when the Thai officials decided to revert to the original sentences handed down, which meant that instead of considering him as an inmate with a numbered sentence, Garth was treated according to his life imprisonment status. This meant he would have to wait eight years before the process of repatriation could even begin.

It wasn't just Garth who was affected; there were many other American convicts who had thought they would be back in America in the near future. The return of those extra four years was worse than any kind of short-lived torture. The men were striving to keep their sanity. Garth had already witnessed several other inmates lose their mind in Bang Kwang, and, consequently, had trained himself to approach each day as a learning experience. He was eating just enough to keep himself alive and disease free. The over-crowding of the cells meant that sickness spread like wild fire amongst the weak. With his embassy's assistance he supplemented his daily ration of poorly cooked rice and cabbage with tuna fish. There was also the worry that he was still surrounded by drugs and users and, naturally, found it impossible not to satisfy his habit, especially since he had not received any help or rehabilitation in the prison system. In fact he had become hooked on heroin in order to cope with his dreadful existence in the prison. He needed to get out of there as quickly as possible. He had suffered a terrible blow when his beloved mother died in 2000, far away from his prison cell. He had also lost a couple of his cellmates, one to freedom and one to death, which I suppose could also be perceived as a freedom from the walls of Bang Kwang.

He had introduced me to Tom J. Auer, an Austrian convict, who had become a close friend of his. They had plenty in common; they shared a cell, drugs and a love for music. My heart sank when Garth first mentioned Tom to me. He said he was a Satanist.

'Terrific,' I thought, 'that's all he needs. Sharing drugs with the devil himself.'

Naturally, I envisioned a monster of a guy with horns and a dark, demonic character, and weakly responded to any funny stories that involved Demon Tom—that is, until I met him in the visiting area. He was lovely! He was tall alright, with a craggy face and soft, grey-blue eyes and a kind smile. I liked him and trusted him immediately. I didn't actually visit him officially; all our communication was passed through Garth or made during brief interchanges in the visiting room. I remember writing once to Garth and remarking that if the Devil was so bad and strong, why did Tom also need to take heroin? He roared with laughter when he heard that and the next time our paths crossed at the prison he smiled mischievously and said, 'Susan, I just need to be a heroin addict for a bit, and then I'll stop.'

True to his word, Tom got clean and has been ever since, having no desire whatsoever for drugs anymore.

He was an artist and drew me a starfish one day, colouring it in with coffee. I reckoned there was a lot of sweetness underneath all that devil stuff.

I was delighted to be able to do him a large favour. His eight years were almost up and a couple of months before his release he heard I was going to visit my family in Australia. He asked me if I could bring him back an Akubra hat, as he wanted to be wearing one for his release day. I never thought to ask him how he knew about this famous accessory. Now, if you have ever seen an Australian drama set in the outback you will know this hat. They are a traditional Aussie hat since the early 1900s and are loved for their durability and comfort. They have an extra wide brim to protect against the scorching sun and heavy rain. Rachel Ward wore one in that famous Australian series, *The Thornbirds*, based on the Colleen McCullough best-selling novel. Anyway, Tom gave me the cash and I walked the streets of Melbourne determined to fetch him the best one for his money. I got him a chocolate brown one and chanced my arm at the shop's till by looking for a discount since it was going to an inmate in Bang Kwang who had just obtained his freedom after eight long years. The girl looked bored and unmoved as she refused to give me or Tom a reduction.

Garth told me that he basically showered and slept in the hat after I gave it to him. I was so glad that I was at the prison the day he received his marching orders. I was standing with Garth and some others and watched Tom being escorted from the bowels of the prison to the entrance. He looking like a man who had been handed a precious second chance and his smile could be clearly seen from a distance. I couldn't help giggling when I saw his 'freedom outfit' of long pants, boots, safari shirt and, of course, his Akubra hat. It was the first time I witnessed someone white leave the prison and I couldn't contain myself. I ran through the beautifully, manicured bushes—possibly taking one or two with me—and I practically threw myself on top of him. We were both in tears and hugged one another. He kept saying to me, over and over again, 'Susan, I'm a free man. A free man. I'm a free man.'

The guard coughed testily and looked like he was going to interrupt us but Tom just turned to him and firmly said, 'No! I'm a free man now.'

The guard nodded sheepishly and backed off. Then he turned back to me and laughed.

'And do you know what else Susan? God is my main guy now.'

He hugged me once more and went on his way, gaily waving to all and sundry. Fortunately, it wasn't the last time I ever heard from him. Throughout the years he has sent me money and gifts for the inmates, especially Thais he left behind in Bang Kwang. He had the strength to deal with his past and embrace it. I knew that I could contact him if the need came up for cash for those he had chosen to support after his departure. There are others who don't want to hear from me because of what I remind them of, which I completely understand.

Tom was one of the few success stories to come out of Bang Kwang. Dtui's was a sadder story and I don't expect everyone to understand why I befriended, and cared about, him. He was just out of his teens when he was arrested, with his pal, for several brutal robberies that involved their victims being badly beaten and even killed. I don't condone his behaviour but I do believe in redemption, in people being worked on so they can have a second bash at life. When Dtui arrived in prison he had nothing. He was penniless so couldn't afford to supplement the meagre and unpleasant food rations, or buy some bedding or toiletries from the prison shop. As a result of his stricken circumstances he ended up becoming a Samurai in the prison. The Samurai are like hired killers; they carry out the dirty work for the prison Mafioso or 'Big Legs' as they are known. The inmates who become Samurai are usually 'prison orphans'. Their families have stopped caring for them and since they then have no ties with the outside world they have no hope and nothing to live for. Therefore, they don't care about anyone or anything, including themselves. Dtui hung out with 10 other fearsome guys. They provided a kind of support system for one another. The 11 of them were heroin addicts and all shared the one needle which eventually led to Dtui losing his 10 mates to AIDS while he remained HIV positive.

He had a motto: 'Evil never dies,' but I found him to be inspirational. He was like a grasshopper; thin, wiry and was always jumping around fuelled by bags of energy. His enthusiasm was boundless and he became a close friend of Garth and me. Another close inmate friend taught him how to play and make guitars and they frequently had me search all of Bangkok for several ingredients and material. They planned to go into business together as soon as they got out. It was fantastic that he should find, within Bang Kwang, an alternative to a life of crime and something that he genuinely loved doing. Dtui differed from other Thais in that he was very confident. If I told him to let me know how I could help him he immediately told me what he needed. Other Thais probably thought him to be rude and cheeky but I found his assertiveness a breath of fresh air. He was very suited to westerners and enjoyed their company.

Garth and I wanted to try and get our hands on some Anti-Retroviral to treat his condition. He appeared to be in good health and I managed to have his blood tested where he was given a positive report. The company who made the Anti-Retroviral hadn't yet sold the rights in Thailand and, consequently, thousands infected with HIV were dying. When it finally was made available in Thailand it cost $25 a month, which I just couldn't afford, and it was restricted to a 'lucky' few. Dtui wouldn't have qualified even if I had been able to buy it. All I could do was bring him in food and treats to keep him relatively healthy.

He, in turn, was able to reward our friendship with one great deed. Garth was in trouble for heroin possession in prison. He had been sent in a package and, according to prison rules, had signed for it before he could open it and see what it was. Dtui was permitted to go to court in Garth's defence, to explain to the judge that he witnessed Garth signing for the package before he discovered what he had signed for, as was the norm. It would be fair to say that he got as much out of the experience as Garth did.

It was the first time in 12 years that he had been outside of the prison and he was like an over-excited child in the prison van. He gazed out the window for the entire journey, gasping over how much Bangkok had changed since he last saw it. He was equally fascinated by all the pretty girls he saw and the fashions of the day. He was also immensely proud that he could help his friends out. This may have been the first time that he was in a position to make a real, positive difference to someone else. I thrusted some chocolate cake at him, his favourite, as he was put in the van, and he almost inhaled it he ate it so fast.

He didn't have an easy time of it in Bang Kwang but, if nothing else, he was a survivor. He had been seen injecting heroin by one of the Blue Shirts. These are the inmates who 'assist' the prison guards in their work. While some of them are really nice people and just want to get through their time in prison, some of them are unpopular, and for good reasons. Some abuse and capitalise on their position horrifically. This one guy began to hassle Dtui, wanting money or he would inform on his drug use. He constantly ambushed Dtui and roughed him over in his increasingly menacing demand for money. One morning the guy went too far and a very stressed Dtui reached the end of his patience; he lunged at the guy and, intentionally or not, killed him.

In that moment he knew that he had just brought a whole lot of trouble down on his head as the other Blue Shirts and guards would be out for revenge. He also knew, without a doubt, that they would kill him as they basically had the run of the prison. But he had a plan. He took to carrying a shard of glass and watched and waited. The attack came a few days later. He was surrounded by a murderous gang, but before they could harm him he beat them to it. He savagely slashed his arms with the glass—everyone knew he was HIV positive—and the disgusted gang melted back into the shadows. There was a tremendous amount of blood everywhere and he had to be hospitalised. When he came out he was moved to another part of the building and was never hassled by the Blue Shirts again. In fact, I think they may have shared a grudging respect for what he did to himself.

He died shortly after. The end came so quickly and was rather unexpected because he had been doing so well. He literally plummeted overnight and when Talya and I tried to visit him we were told that he was too sick. If it had been today he would've received the required medicine but back then there was nothing to be done for him. It was a terrible waste of a young life. I fervently believe that he would have made a huge change in his life and might have found happiness. At the time he was writing to a girl in the women's prison. They had never met but sent each other funny, flirtatious letters. Anything was possible. Garth and I really missed him for a long time after that. So, you can understand why I wanted Garth out of that environment. There's only so much sadness a normal person can take.

I suppose the two guys, Tom and Dtui, reminded me that you can't make quick judgements about someone; everyone has a story and a good side to them. The other thing about Tom's happy ending was that his release illustrated how other countries' treaties were working just fine. It seemed ridiculous that the 'all-powerful' America couldn't get her inmates out of Bang Kwang.

There were a few unfortunate circumstances that didn't help at the time. A strong-willed and efficient woman, Judy, left her post at the American embassy for another job. Her successor left soon after, deciding that she hadn't the heart for the position. Now there were only two Thais at the US embassy; a woman ran the office while a guy visited the prison and kept inmates well informed. They were lovely to deal with but had no power to set priorities within the embassy or push through big decisions.

Alongside this, a minor war erupted on the streets between the Thai government and the drug dealers, and a major campaign got under way to clear the streets of anyone to do with drugs and the business. Releasing foreign drug users and dealers was not part of this new agenda, and the Justice Ministry, Interior Ministry and the Department of Corrections gave the Embassy Transfer Committee the run around. This wasn't helped by the new hardliner Army General who had come to power. From what I could gather, when the other embassies submitted transfer papers to the committee the Thai officials would interrogate the embassies about how the inmate was going to be received back home, and what further punishment would be meted out. Most embassies stated that the inmates would be re-sentenced according to the Receiving States' Law which went some way towards satisfying the Thais. However, the American embassy wouldn't play ball due to being short staffed—there was no authorised representative to address the Thai officials.

Every time the Transfer Committee met for a meeting I would anxiously ring for an update on the American inmates, only to be told that the transfer was 'pending'. This happened several times and I absolutely loathed being the one to tell the guys that their transfer hadn't been processed yet. They must've dreaded my visits at that time. It was awful to sit there and watch these grown men break down. The stress they were under was unfathomable and there was no one to fight for them with the Transfer Committee. I needed to do something, but as usual I had to be sensitive. It was pointless to upset the officials about American drug dealers during the heightened tensions on the streets outside. They would just say no and have a list of reasons ready to support their decision.

The American embassy contacted me and asked for a 4.30pm meeting on a Friday afternoon. This was unusual—to bring me in after office hours—and I was more than a little nervous as I walked through the quiet corridors down to the conference room. I heard whispers from some passing staff, 'That's Susan Aldous, the prison activist.'

I had never heard myself been called that before but it had a nice ring to it. When I entered the room I saw that there was quite a mixture of embassy staff there; mostly women. The Counsel General was there but I didn't speak with her. The meeting was more instrumental in what was left unsaid, rather than what was actually said. I was grilled by a couple of the women; I think they wanted to check my sincerity and knowledge of the situation. They asked me about the transfer treaty, and, without telling me, I was left to understand that the treaty had broken down irretrievably thanks, in the American's opinion, to the Thais. Some 60 names had been cleared for transfer while the remaining nine were 'pending'. I wasn't an official and therefore could only be told so much, which wasn't much at all. Their eyes were pleading with me while their language was corporate and correct. When it was finished, a few of us walked outside together, and once we left the building I found myself blurting out the question I'd been waiting to ask:

'So, what are you really trying to tell me? There is no treaty? These guys can't go home any time soon?'

Some of the women teared up as they made their automatic responses, 'We are not at liberty to divulge that information to you.'

But, they just had.

In hindsight I think the treaty broke down because the US wasn't backing the inmates; the Ambassador didn't want to stand on the Thais' hardliner toes. Their priority was to keep a smooth diplomatic relationship with the Thai government and to be seen to support their war on drugs. That's just my opinion. Whatever the reason was, I felt I had been handed the baton, by the American embassy, to run alone down a potentially treacherous path. I had to watch my back. I was a foreign woman with no legal rights or privileges. I wasn't even American. I was still followed by the police from time to time and I still had enemies at the prison. All in all, it wouldn't take much to set me up on a drugs charge, so the responsibility was, potentially, life threatening for me. I walked the streets of Bangkok feeling ill and claustrophobic at my precarious situation. Furthermore, the thought of returning to tell the guys what I had learnt did not appeal to me in the least. And, of course, I thought about myself and Garth and how another year or two seemed like a very, very long time indeed.

I needed a plan of action. I went on Amnesty International's website and I also studied Green Peace literature to see how they initiated their campaigns. If anything was going to be achieved it would most likely have to come from the embassy, even if it was just a courteous phone call. After all, Thailand needed American business, so we really had the advantage when you think about it.

One American, Jeff, was a wine importer and frequently made time to visit American inmates at Bang Kwang. I contacted him because I knew that he had contacts in CNN. However, bringing in the TV station would be a last resort; I would try the less flamboyant tactics first. I contacted every single American inmate eligible for transfer and explained the situation as positively as I could. I also told them that I needed their help and urged them to write to any influential people that they knew back in the States, including their local representatives. The idea was to *politely* pressurise the American Ambassador with tons of letters and enquiries about the prisoners, forcing him *nicely* to do something about it. I stressed to the inmates that there was no call for nastiness or threatening letters—the more professional everything was the more impact the campaign would have.

It was slow work but we were getting results. Jeff was invited to a Royal function and was delighted to find himself seated next to the American Ambassador and his wife. As soon as it was appropriate, Jeff respectfully asked the Ambassador about the treaty.

The Ambassador replied, 'Don't worry, we are well aware of the situation and we're going to do something about it.'

This was heartening news indeed.

Shortly after there was another meeting of the Transfer Committee and the nine Americans, amongst others, were on the agenda. The meeting was scheduled to take place on a Friday but was then moved to the following Tuesday, as Monday was a public holiday. It was a miracle it was even held on the Tuesday as meetings were frequently postponed for months. I was really nervous because I knew that if the committee ran out of time, whoever they didn't get to would have to wait for the next meeting, three months later.

The Americans submitted their papers with a little note from their ambassador attached. It worked a charm and I dissolved into joyful tears when I received the phone call, the very same day, to tell me that all the guys had made it. I practically skipped into Bang Kwang on the Wednesday to tell them the good news. Everyone was jumping up and down and embracing one another when three embassy officials arrived to tell the men what I had just told them. It was a huge triumph and proved what could be done if lots of people work together to attain a common goal. Garth and I grinned foolishly at one another—a couple on the brink of a new life together in the 'land of the free'.

I had made a decision long before that day; if he was ever permitted a transfer back to the States Talya and I would leave Thailand to make our lives with him as a family. It was like a beautiful dream come true, a time of hope and celebration. The last six months of his imprisonment in Bang Kwang flew by with both of us elated and giddy with excitement and plans. We wrote countless letters to one another outlining what we both hoped for from our new life in America. Garth looked the best I had ever seen him. He had lived up to his promise of coming off heroin before his release and I thought his newfound energy and colour stemmed from happiness.

I sent an email out to all of our supporters:

*

OK folks. It's time to put the champagne on ice and to start laughing and crying simultaneously while wildly jumping up and down a few times thanking God! Garth and seven other American inmates are heading home on 7 December. Yep, you read that right! It's finally happening.

I can hardly believe it myself, in fact I don't think I really will until we are assured that they have taken off and flown well out of Thailand's airspace.

It's just indescribable how much of a battle this long, faith-testing, sanity-destroying process has been. Even the embassy staff have been unusually flabbergasted at the amount of time and obstacles that have had to be overcome to make this transfer work.

Ha, they will not tell us just what type of aircraft that they are using to transfer folk outta here, but who cares! A kite would do, as long as it gets them out safely.

For the returnees, hot showers, real beds, filling food, telephones and reasonable treatment will be hard to adjust to I suspect, but definitely well deserved.

Thanks, one and all, for your many years of loyal care and support. It's kept us going and it sure has meant a great deal. How wonderfully the light of true friendship has been contrasted on this very dark background of suffering.

*

That summer Talya and I arrived in Australia for our every-second-year month long visit. I brought a letter from Garth. It was time to tell the family about my relationship. I hadn't told them before because I knew that they'd worry. I gathered everyone into the lounge of my parent's house and told them I was getting married. Their smiles and shouts of delight crumpled when I told them who the groom was. Typically, my parents didn't let me down. They were obviously worried but told me that they trusted my good judgement. Garth wrote a long letter to my father, detailing his love for Talya and me while appreciating any ambiguity and concern due to his circumstances. What with our immediate move to America it could prove some time before he met them in person and he desperately hoped to allay any major fears and misconceptions. I still have the letter, which ends:

*

All in all, I want for you to rest assured that I indeed have your daughter's best interests at heart and that she and Tally have found a source of love, happiness and caring which is truly unrivalled.

It seemed almost too good to be true. I had found the man of my dreams, who cherished my daughter and I, and on top of that we would move to America where I believed I could continue setting up projects with Garth on his eventual release. We had spoken about maybe heading to Central America and working side by side together. Talya would have a full-time dad who was as devoted to her as she was to him. While I may have experienced some sadness at leaving Thailand, she was absolutely raring to see America.

Our excitement mounted as Garth's transfer day approached. I did try to marry him before he left Bang Kwang. A young journalist friend of mine, a New Zealander, loved the romance of our story and wanted to write about us with the angle, 'love behind bars'. She encouraged me to chase the paperwork for having the wedding in the prison. I think it would have been a good thing for the other prisoners. Most of the guys seemed to thrive on my relationship with Garth—it was a positive thing that such a horrible place could bring two people together and foster their love through years of prison visits. Also, I would've liked to involved the guards I was friendly with, and perhaps it would be 'mud in your eye' for the mean guards who teased us at every opportunity.

I went to the Foreign Affair Ministry and got all the documents translated and did everything that I was asked. But, it was not to be. There was always some silly excuse. I felt I was being thwarted at every level, no matter how much research I did and how many papers I filled out. Afterwards I wondered if the guards and prison officials were trying to protect me. The whole episode over the heroin package left a bad taste in the guards' mouths and once more some of them tried to convey their apprehension over my choice of husband. Of course, they knew more than me and were a lot more pessimistic—or realistic—about Garth's ability to kick drugs forever. The heroin I had accepted, just because of where he was spending his days, months, years. I had nodded in understanding when Tom told me that he just needed to be a heroin addict until he knew he was leaving Bang Kwang. I didn't agree with it but I convinced myself that it just had to be. Drugs were so easy to get in the prison and if you weren't drinking, you needed something else to cope with that life. Many inmates over the years of the prison's history had literally gone insane—this was a real threat that you had to protect yourself from.

Anyway, I had asked Garth to kick the habit and he had in the six months before his transfer date. I was so proud of him and enjoyed the new junk-free Garth who was full of energy and enthusiasm. What I didn't know, and what the guards presumably did, was that the spring in Garth's step was thanks largely to the speed he was taking as a substitute for the heroin. As they say, 'ignorance is bliss.' I was busy packing me and Talya up. I had been reading up on America and floated ideas like moving to Costa Rica or Mexico. I wouldn't be leaving for America with Garth; there was so much still to be done, and besides, he was heading to the Metropolitan Detention Centre in Los Angeles for a couple of months.

One more problem had to be dealt with as the men busied themselves for their return to America. No aeroplane would bring them home. This was the aftermath of 9/11 so the American airlines refused to transport the prisoners, even when the US government told them that there would be a full prison escort of six armed guards in service. It was a worrying time but it was all sorted in the end. A plane was booked, and not just any plane. Before collecting the

American prisoners it had dropped off illegal Cambodian emigrants back to Cambodia. The emigrants had been caught, with expired green cards, in America and had spent the previous six months in an American immigration centre, waiting to be deported. Only the story wasn't as black and white as it seemed. I later found out, via *The New York Times*, that these Cambodians included children who had been born in the US. Therefore, they had never seen Cambodia and had little or no knowledge of the language; they considered themselves, instead, to be American and had been forcefully uprooted from the only home that they had known. They and their families had no rights or say in where they wanted to live. It was a deplorable situation.

***

That long-awaited Friday, transfer day, had finally arrived. I was so excited I couldn't eat a morsel of food. My friend Mary and I galloped down to the prison just as the five guys, including Garth, were being lead out, still in their chains. Garth hadn't slept in three days and his eyes were as round as saucers—from the speed no less. They were dressed in civilian clothes, with proper shoes, and they all looked scrubbed up and utterly ecstatic. They were all big, tall men, but looked as nervous and unsure of themselves as young schoolboys being allowed out by themselves for the first time. They seemed to hover in front of the van like uneasy wall flowers at a raucous party. My heart just melted at the sight of them.

Mary and I stampeded through the bushes and ran at them, hugging and kissing them, reminding them that this was a joyous event. The guards didn't try to stop us. I think we two girls brought an element of normality to the situation and the guys could release their emotions with flowing tears and words of thanks. Garth put his arms around me and lifted me clean off the ground. I buried my face in his neck and whispered to him through my tears. Then the guys were led onto the prison van. Chavoret was in charge of the transfer and I smiled my biggest smile at him while asking if Mary and I could travel with them? However, Chavoret was a stickler for the rules and told me, through gritted teeth, 'No you can't. This is official business.'

It was worth a try.

As the guys were being settled into the van Mary and I flagged down a taxi. Once the van took off we gave chase all the way to the immigration centre. The driver enjoyed our hysterics as he speeded up in order to drive alongside the van at one point. The guys almost had their noses pressed up to the windows, taking in all the sights after so many years behind bars. It was a beautiful December morning, Pearl Harbour Day in the US, and the sky was high in the sky. Bangkok had never appeared so beautiful and exciting as I looked at it anew through the eyes of the Americans.

When we arrived at the building we had a few moments with the men outside. There were a couple of journalists waiting to see me and Garth. Photographs taken of us enjoying ice-cream cups side by side appeared the next day in *The Bangkok Post*. Then, it was time for the men to go inside. Mary and I were told that we couldn't follow.

'No way!'

I thought to myself and headed up to smile at the deputy commander and asked him nicely if I could please, please go in to be with Garth. He couldn't resist me, and Mary and I ran to catch up with the others. The guys were in a cell and

I squatted on the other side so that I could kiss and embrace Garth. We weren't going to have any time together so there was no way I was going to wait politely on the streets and miss possible precious moments like this. I would kick myself afterwards if I just obeyed silly orders.

The prisoners were then led into another room where they were met by some Thai officials and two other female prison visitors who had cared for the women inmates for some time. They lined up to have their photos and fingerprints taken. You wouldn't believe the amount of administration involved in a prison transfer. I was delighted to see that food had been provided and there was even salsa music playing in the background. The volunteers, inmates and myself all wanted a party atmosphere and there certainly was plenty to celebrate. I had the briefest few seconds alone in the corner of the room with Garth and we hurriedly told one another that we loved each other and exchanged rings.

All too briefly the suits arrived—two important officials from the embassy. I didn't know them but they frowned at us, their misgivings over our presence clear for all too see. I held my breath, thinking that they were going to say that the transfer wasn't going ahead. The prisoners had to take their seats on the other side of the room and we weren't allowed near them. My panic turned to delight when the officials opened up their bags and handed around Kentucky Fried Chicken meals as their last goodwill gesture.

It was time for me to leave. I blew Garth a kiss and headed outside, elated and sad at the same time. It was weird to leave that party atmosphere and simply head back out onto the streets and continue on with my day. I was going to miss Garth terribly and hoped that the next few months would go by very quickly.

***

The guy from the embassy rang me later that evening to assure me that the men were on their way home safe and sound. The following morning the phone woke me. It was a very excited friend of mine telling me that I was on the front page of the newspapers. I was barely awake as I stumbled over to my computer to check out the news page on the internet. It took me quite a few minutes to remember I was stark naked and in full view of some neighbours who were breakfasting on their balcony and doing their utmost to pretend that they couldn't see me. I waved my apologies and returned to my room to put on a sarong.

Garth arrived back in America on 9 December 2002. He spent 90 days in the detention centre in LA. On 8 January he was interviewed about his Thai crime and made a statement fully accepting responsibility for his actions:

'I pleaded guilty and I knew what I was doing. However, I did not travel knowing in advance that I would smuggle drugs. I wish it had never happened. I never had a chance to say goodbye to my mother. I am sorry I committed the offence.'

When he was asked what he would do following his release he said that the first thing he would do would be to go to Monterey and meet up with his family. It was agreed that he would move in with his brother, Rogan, and his girlfriend Angie. They had formally declared that they were ready to provide Garth with room and board and assistance with settling back into the community.

Over the next few months I continued with my prison visits. When I arrived at the visitor's registration room I kept automatically adding Garth's name to the list of prisoners I had come to see, which made the guards smirk. It was just strange to think that he was back in America now but I also felt good about the fact that without a boyfriend in Bang Kwang, at the mercy of the guards, I didn't feel so vulnerable anymore. Nobody could make me uncomfortable and I didn't have to worry about my behaviour causing him any hassle. I was tying up loose ends and had sent Talya to spend some time with her dad's second family, her half-siblings. She really impressed me with her maturity at this point and told me that it would be better if she followed me to America a couple of months later, thereby letting me and Garth get properly acquainted and settled before her arrival. It made perfect sense to me when she said it and I'll always be grateful and proud of her for this.

There was only a couple of suitcases of stuff. I had given away everything else and then moved into a hotel for the last week or so. Joe and Lena, good friends of mine, had lent me most of my furniture to date so I returned it to them. Everything else I gave away, including a most beautiful coffee-table, hard backed book about Mother Theresa, with lots of fantastic photos. I had received this as a present the previous year from one of my dearest Aussie friends, and found it inspiring—she had always been a role model of mine and I would've loved to have met her. I was delighted to pass it on and make a present of it to my good friend Nina. She was heavily involved with most of my projects and would continue to make prison visits after I was gone.

In fact there were plenty of people to take over the work. Most of them had been doing it all along. I had such a good friend in Buzz, a retired, well-heeled attorney from Pheonix, Arizona in the US. He had already given so much of his time and resources, especially in regards to the Naval Psychiatric Wards and Drug Rehab Unit and was 100% reliable, which was why I was going to ask him to take over my role there. I didn't get to ask him, however, as he approached me first to offer himself instead. He'll never know how grateful I was to him for that.

Dr Shan, a British forensic psychiatrist, was also a good mate. I had first met him in Klong Prem prison and he introduced me to his friend, Dr Bob, a retired dentist. The two men were doing Trojan work in the prisons and were going to take over the glasses project in Klong Prem, ensuring that the elderly inmates received eye tests and spectacles as required, which is still on-going to this day. They were also involved in Bang Kwang, offering free psychiatry and dental care to the inmates. By this stage there were also plenty of voluntary prison visitors who filled the gaps. You can't imagine what one simple visit does for an inmate in Bang Kwang. You can bring him nutritious food, like bananas or carrot cake, or even a bottle of shower gel or deodorant and chat to them about the outside world, just making them feel human and a part of the world again.

Basically there were plenty of people to cover my absence. I was experiencing the same feelings that I had when I was making my preparations to leave Australia for Asia. In one way it felt that my time in Thailand was up and it was right that I should be moving on. Some of the old Thai officials that I had known and worked with were being replaced with new, tougher characters and I missed the men of old. Also there was a horrible atmosphere in Bangkok now thanks to the government stepping up its war on the drug trade. The police were arresting suspected junkies and dealers willy nilly, or else shooting them dead in the streets.

worry about. In return for his service and personal risk Aree would receive pocket money, US$8,000, return flight tickets, train tickets to travel around Europe and another $8,000 on his return to Thailand.

Aree wasn't easily persuaded and he told Ah Chi that he would have to think about it. A few weeks later Aree had almost forgotten about the offer but his luck took an unfortunate turn when he ended up undergoing surgery on his stomach after days of copious vomiting and fainting at work from the pain. He needed two operations, which left him physically weak —too weak for work. Consequently, he was in dire financial straits. As soon as he was able, he sought out Ah Chi to take him up on his offer. He felt he had no choice.

He ended up on death row in Bang Kwang prison, with 300 inmates squeezed into 16 cells. There was little space to move and Aree was struck by the paleness and listlessness of his fellow cell-mates. Three times a week, for one hour only, the inmates were allowed out of their cells for fresh air, to collect their food rations, and wash themselves and their clothes. The water was pumped from a nearby river and was usually dirty and full of a variety of insects. The insects also turned up in the food; no matter how hungry you are it still difficult to swallow the unrecognisable vegetables, which have been soaked in rotten fish soup, and the accompanying brown rice that wriggles on the plate thanks to the busy insects laying their eggs or defecating in it. He was driven to picking up and washing every single grain of rice to make sure that he wasn't eating worms or larvae. Naturally, he suffered greatly with his ulcers and was prevented from receiving the proper medicine that he asked a translator to send in to him.

I asked him once what he missed the most about the outside world and he replied;

'Everything. In the daytime you can talk with people and you are always surrounded by the other inmates, yet you can still feel very lonely. In the night time I miss seeing the sky full of stars and the moon. I miss seeing nature; life in here is so unnatural.'

The biggest thing I could do for Aree was to feed him. Every day I went to the Non bakery and they kindly gave me heavy bags of leftover food—so heavy with cakes, pastries and bread, that I strained my neck and arms carrying these bags to the prison. Then, I saw that the local Pizza Hut did an 'All you can eat' night every Tuesday. The manager and staff were horrified when I marched in and asked them what they were going to do with the food that wasn't eaten. They wondered at a white, foreign woman being so poor and desperate that she had to beg for leftover food. It turned out that the food just gets thrown out at the end of the evening. When I explained that it was for inmates at the prison they gladly let me take away the uneaten pizzas—that was another heavy bag. You just can't imagine how magnificent a cold pizza or stale pastry is to a starving, demoralised prisoner who spends most of his meal time removing insects from his dinner. It makes him feel human again to be eating, as it were, proper, civilised food.

One time I scored really well on the food front. My friend Mila and her husband worked with the Canadian embassy in Bangkok, and she also frequently visited prisoners in Bang Kwang. She invited me to a party to celebrate Canada Day, which was held in a fancy hotel in Bangkok. It was a great party with lots of people, party games and lots of gorgeous food, from a huge selection of roast meats to sweet cakes.

I sat with embassy staff at a table and they were asking me about my work. I filled them in and made strong hints that they could be doing the same things in their positions. Anyway, there was a tonne of food left over so Mila and I asked the staff if we could take it. The manager refused, initially, saying that it was against hotel policy. I think the staff had their eye on it instead. Mila and I went to work on him and he, eventually, gave in, just to be rid of us.

Well, there was so much food that the staff had to get me a trolley so I could put all the bags into a taxi; I could barely fit into the passenger seat of the car. I paid the driver extra so he would help me carry the bags into the reception desk at Bang Kwang. The checking-in process is slow and it was a while before all the bags were cleared to be brought in, involving me running back and forth from the desk to the visitor's section. But it was more than worth it to the guys inside.

Aree tells me that his life has improved considerably since I came into his life and he is certainly one of the people who keeps me going when I'm feeling low. He was very close to Garth and me, so close that we 'adopted' him. There's something very special about this guy and I rely on him a lot to help me with other inmates I can't reach in Bang Kwang. He humbles me with his dignity and sense of pride, which remains untouched even when he is struggling around in his heavy chains. He has managed to maintain his sanity through his long years of imprisonment, on death row, in solitary confinement, and in an over-crowded cell, by cooking for a western inmate who has since been released. It has been a long, lonely struggle for him since he is one of a large number of prisoners who hears, and receives, absolutely nothing from his family.

He's an intelligent, thoughtful, young man who has never complained once to me and has stoically remained drugs-free even when all around him are developing habits to cope with imprisonment.

There is no way on this good earth that he should be serving a life sentence and I've worked hard to draw attention to his plight. He feels much more positive knowing that he has people out here who support and care for him. He receives lots of letters now, mostly from people he has never met, and even receives gifts of books. It has given him a new lease of life. If only his own embassy could be that forth-coming. I can't mention his nationality (he's not Thai) since he's still in Bang Kwang but, suffice to say, they have only visited him a couple of times and that was way back in the 1990s.

My work is made a lot easier by the amount of good folk who write to me and ask to be put in contact with someone who needs a friend. All I have to do is pair them up with a prisoner who will especially thrive on receiving letters or gifts of toiletries and books. It is a big responsibility however, since I have to be sure not to recommend someone who is out to deceive. Nevertheless, it's hugely rewarding for everyone involved and I would urge anyone reading this book to contact their embassy in Thailand, or go on the internet to the excellent website www.foreignprisoners.com if they feel they could write a few letters to someone who hasn't seen the night sky in, literally, years. Readers can also look at my webgroup which can be found at http://groups.yahoo.com/group/onelifeatatime, to read past newsletters and to see how changes in th eprison are taking place.

Just imagine being banged up for the rest of your life. Apart from the obvious things like loss of freedom, bad food and absolutely no personal space, try to imagine the horrific boredom of the day-to-day existence. If you can do that, then you can surely appreciate the difference made by receiving a letter.

***

I first met Peter when he was holed up in Building 2 in Bang Kwang with Garth. I was introduced to him in the visiting area and took to him immediately. He, in turn, introduced me to his wife, Anne, and also his parents. Back then the visiting centre was out in the open and you really had to shout to be heard by the prisoner you were visiting. The regular visitors would greet one another like old friends and would discreetly wink in comradeship and nod in the direction of 'fair-weather visitors'—the earnest back-packers, colourful Nigerian visitors and saintly-looking missionaries.

Anne, along with inmates and families alike, used to call the hippie back-packers 'the banana visitors', because they turned up to give bananas to inmates as if they were caged monkeys in a zoo. I remember one loud, obnoxious American guy lambaste the prisoner he was visiting, for the first time, calling him a 'freaking idiot' for ending up in Bang Kwang—how he thought that this was helpful or, even, news to the guy is beyond me.

Then, there are the other misguided young male visitors who obviously don't know what to talk about, so they regale the inmate with tales of their Bangkok sexual exploits. It is like they are following the rules of some underground travel guide to Bangkok;

a) sleep with a Thai prostitute,

b) visit an inmate in Bang Kwang.

I listened in disbelief one day to a young guy loudly boast about how he refused to pay Thai women for sex; he always got freebies. Ugh! There was no sympathy or interest in whoever he was visiting. Not all of them, fortunately, have this attitude; others would come out visibly upset after their visit and would make a generous donation out of their limited travelling budget. Other people have continued to make a difference after their visit. They mightn't be able to afford to send money but they campaign and draw attention to an inmate when they return home and write frequent letters to let their compatriot know that he hasn't been forgotten.

But, as in most walks of life, the vulnerable have to be protected from the scams. I was asked one day to help an inmate who was in need of a life-saving operation. There was a campaign already in place and thousands of dollars had been collected for the prisoner. I met up with some of those involved and asked why they didn't contact the guy's embassy and the Department of Corrections to get the operation organised. Then I found out there was no illness, no life-saving operation required, and not only that but the embassy—which shall remain nameless—were in on the scam with the prisoner. They were going to take a cut out of the money raised. I discovered all this after a guy from the embassy arranged to meet me to discuss the case. When we met, in a public place, he grabbed my breasts—something which I'm sure he has done many times before with other unsuspecting girls.

After I went to the DOC to hurry along the process, I finally met with the 'sick' guy himself to tell him what I had organised and he completely freaked out at me. I knew then it was all a scam and walked away. I have a policy that I don't get involved in things like this. It's not my place or duty to expose fraudsters. I have to look after my personal safety on the outside. I did manage, nevertheless, to deter one generous, wealthy Australian woman from pouring thousands of dollars into this guy's fund. She wrote to me to ask about the operation and, without bad-mouthing the guy, I advised her that there were more deserving projects that her money could make a huge difference to. She ended up sponsoring quite a few projects over the next few years and proved not only to be a great material supporter but an emotional and spiritual inspiration.

We were the 'banana brigade', on the other hand, the ones who did the real work—carrying out requests for inmates, cooking meals for them and doing their shopping. After Garth and I had fallen in love, Anne and I forged a special bond visiting our jailbirds. We swapped romantic tit-bits that we wouldn't have dared tell anyone else. I loved hearing how they met. They were both dating each other's best friends when they met at a reception for a political cause. They became instant friends and couldn't quite believe it when they found themselves falling for one another. Sadly, they each lost their best friend!

Visits can be extremely difficult on families and loved ones. I've lost count of the amount of times that I've held distressed mothers, sisters and wives. Bang Kwang is the last place you want someone you care about to end up. I knew a mother who had to literally watch her young son dying in front of her—there was nothing she could do. He contracted HIV and was given the fatal diagnosis upon entering the prison. Other parents re-mortgage their homes to try and get their children out of prison by hiring the best lawyer they can afford. It is inevitable, and even necessary, that regular visitors start to support one another and pass on smiles and words of encouragement. We're a little like soldiers fighting a personal war in a strange land and if one falls, we all fall. I think I was a help to Anne on days when she felt low, while she certainly inspired me by sticking by her husband. I've seen men being deserted by their ashamed or sensitive wives who find it easier to pretend that they are widows.

I asked Peter to illustrate how harsh life could be inside the prison. He told me a story about a Thai inmate who made his living in Bang Kwang by repairing electrical equipment for the other inmates. He relied on a prison guard he knew to go to the shops and buy him the parts he needed. Then this guard was transferred so he had to approach another one who turned out to be an alcoholic. The inevitable happened. The inmate needed a part to repair a guy's walkman and he gave the guard money to get it. That was the last he saw of his money. The guard kept coming up with excuses as to why he didn't have the electronic part. After some persistence on the part of the inmate the guard confessed that he had spent his money on drink, saying, 'Hey, shit happens!'

The inmate went away and simmered. He snapped a short while later. He spotted the guard reporting for work and grabbed an iron bar. He bashed the guard on the head and he went down. Blue Shirts jumped the Thai inmate. They dragged him to the supervisor's office and left him lying outside. The supervisor came out with a bamboo cane and proceeded to beat the guy all over the body. This was just the beginning. Peter's account tells how it went:

*

The guards took turns—two or three at a time—to beat the inmate, using batons, canes and even their boots. When one guard tired, another took his place. After two hours the beating abated, temporarily, until fresh guards from the other buildings took over. The Blue Shirts stood on guard around the scene, making sure that the rest of the inmates didn't try to intervene.

We westerners, in particular, pleaded in vain with the guards to stop. The shock of witnessing this brutality was too much for one western guy and he collapsed with a heart attack. It took some time to get a guard to agree to bring him down to the infirmary but it was too late. He died.

We heard later that his embassy had actually brought him the prescribed medicine for his heart but the guards had delayed in giving it to him.

The Thai inmate was left lying in his own blood until the following afternoon when he was brought to the infirmary. We all assumed he would die but months later, to our surprise, we saw him hobbling slowly from the punishment building. He was a broken man and would live out the rest of his life as a cripple.

*

Like a lot of inmates Peter turned to heroin and he and Garth would snort it together. They would drink Pepsi afterwards to get rid of the taste—apparently it's an acquired taste. Peter is a tall guy, 6ft 4", and when he lost about 50 kilos he looked like a skeletal prisoner of war. He also lost most of his teeth to heroin. When he first got busted for possession of drugs, Anne was so angry that she didn't visit him for almost a year. She told him that she wouldn't visit him again until he got clean. I don't know how she did it but she did and it probably saved him. He battled his addiction and beat it; not an easy thing to do in Bang Kwang. He got his hair cut, got his teeth done, put on weight, started working out and became a fitness fanatic. They got married behind bars. I asked her to tell me about the early years of Peter's incarceration, and this is what she told me:

*

I was at university and working part-time and Peter went with some friend for a short holiday in Thailand. I came home from work one afternoon to see two policemen in civilian clothes waiting to speak to me ... They told me that Peter had been arrested for drug-trafficking and was being detained in a Thai prison.

They informed me that drug-related crimes often resulted in a death sentence.

During those first years there were so many practical things to take care of and that was where I concentrated my resources after trying to just survive and keep Peter's spirit up through letters. I had to locate an English-speaking lawyer in Bangkok, prepare the support documents for his trial, then the papers for the appeal, all the while struggling to understand the whole Thai prison and trial system, raising the money to visit him, establish contacts with our embassy and the ministry of foreign affairs in our country. Not one day went by without my writing at least one letter to get support to get him home. At the time there was no transfer agreement with our country. Together with a small group of relatives we managed to bug and create enough interest from the ministry of foreign affairs to start negotiating a transfer agreement with Thailand.

It took a lot of time researching other countries' agreements so that we knew what kind of agreement to push for.

I think I was lucky that I was able to channel my energy, heartache and despair into doing practical stuff. Peter just had to survive, and if one hour felt long in my world it must've felt like years in his.

Some time during all of this Peter developed a serious addiction to drugs—the time behind bars, the waiting and the desperation got to him. I understood, but it was impossible for me to accept and just watch while he slowly disappeared.

I had managed to save enough money to go visit once or twice a year and I knew those visits were what kept us alive and fighting. His addiction was really bad, so I had to give him an ultimatum; I cancelled a Christmas visit and wrote that he had to choose between me or the drugs. It will always be the worst thing that I ever had to do in my life. But love conquers all. Peter beat the habit and has never taken drugs since. I can't imagine how difficult that was for him. Behind bars there were no detoxification programmes, no counselling or support from his peers. He did it completely on his own.

On my first visits to Bang Kwang, sitting outside the prison office waiting for a visit application to be approved, I noticed that there were other westerners among the visitors. I was really surprised as I never expected there could be other westerners in the same situation as me— that someone else would have a husband, brother or father here.

I worked up the courage to go and speak to them and ended up making the closet friends I will ever have, in the shape of a big, friendly Scottish man and his lovely wife, the nicest, blue-eyed, red-haired Aussie, a beautiful but sad French girl, an English woman about my mother's age, and the warm, chatty blond from Melbourne.

My love for my husband made me survive the years of separation but I have no doubt in my heart that those people were the ones who kept me sane.

There were, at that time, around 200 westerners imprisoned in Bang Kwang and we were some of the few relatives who visited, returning year after year, sharing our despair and our little victories—we truly were the 'banana brigade'.

*

As I've said, Anne and I kept each other going. During her visits to Bangkok we always tried to make sure we did something to cheer ourselves up. We swam, went to the movies and took up dancing classes, where we failed miserably to learn how to either salsa or do the cha cha cha very well. One afternoon we arranged to meet for coffee after our visit. There were four of us; another friend of mine, a mother of an inmate, Anne and me. Garth gave me 500 baht along with a note from him and Peter telling us that they would love to be able to take the four of us out on the town, but since they couldn't they wanted to buy us drinks. We were all in tears!

Peter and Anne are still very much happy together, having worked hard to put their Bang Kwang years behind them. After serving his nine years in Bangkok Peter was transferred home to spend another year in prison, and then he was in a half-way house for six months before being finally released on a five-year probation. He started to study for a bachelor degree in the half-way house and graduated this year, and has started teaching at his local university. I asked him if it was difficult to resume a normal life together, and he replied:

*

It actually turned out to be much easier than I had thought. Anne and I have resumed our life together but in a deeper way. We know and love each other deeply and our ordeal has brought us closer together. We know that if we could survive that we can survive anything.

*

CHAPTER TWELVE

I'm only back here in Thailand since 1 May 2006. Once I initiated divorce proceedings my days as a legal inhabitant in America were numbered. This seems to be the general pattern of my life; I have to give up something good in order to achieve something positive. Though maybe that's a universal pattern, is it not? And aside from my heart-breaking, humiliating experience with Garth and my almost bleeding to death, I do have some very fond memories from my years in the States. It's a country I never thought I would visit—let alone make a home there—because its politics and commercialism always discouraged me.

Things I miss about America: I would have to say firstly that I miss the people, from the homeless on the streets to Garth's band mates, to my best friends Larry and Cathy. I thrive with people who are open to discussion and forthright in their opinions and the people I met were always outstandingly honest. Secondly, I would have to say that I miss the American male. Now, before you jump to conclusions, what I miss about the American male is that he can do platonic friendship with women. I made some great male friends in Monterey; far easier than I can here. As much as I love Thailand—my adopted country of 18 of my 26 years abroad—I do have to grit my teeth sometimes. There are a lot of social niceties that must be followed and it's extremely easy to unintentionally offend. Thai men have to be handled carefully or they will get the wrong idea immediately.

For instance, I was visiting the women's prison at Klong Prem several years ago, which was a fair distance from where I was living. A young lawyer I knew to smile at, offered me a lift home, which I gratefully accepted. He asked me all about my work and by the time I reached my front door he gave me his number and expressed an interest in helping me with my projects. A few weeks later he rang to invite me out to dinner. I brought Talya along with me and naively thought about any help he could provide me with.

However, the conversation took a surprising turn when he told me that he had gone back to his village to ask his mother if he could propose to me. I almost choked on my meal while he continued to tell me that he couldn't sleep at nights because he was thinking of me. Talya cracked up, so he decided on a more practical seduction. He told my daughter that he was in love with her mother and he wanted to support and care for us both—for starters he would give us 1,000 baht a month. Talya stopped laughing and began to seriously consider his offer. Then he reached into his pocket and handed her a bundle of notes. It's common practice in Thailand for adults to give children money, but this was really too much. I frantically searched my brain for a polite way to get out of the situation. Finally, I managed to say something like, 'You have to slow down. I love my life and am very married already to my work.'

He seemed to accept that and we continued on with the meal. He rang again to invite me to dinner, this time to meet his boss who wished to see if I would do some work for his law firm. I thought that with the boss' presence I would be safe enough. Again, I brought Talya, who was probably hoping for some more pocket-money from our wealthy friend. I really hit it off with his boss who was fluent in English. He was interested in the prison work I was doing at the time. My would-be lover felt a little excluded during our English conversation so he took Talya over to the play area in the restaurant. As he pushed her on the swing he waxed lyrical again about his love for me. Talya, very matter-of-factly, told him that I wasn't in the least bit interested in him, that I just saw him as a friend and asked would he please 'stop hassling my mum.'

She returned alone to the table eating an ice-cream cone. I asked her where our friend was and she shrugged and said that she had informed him that I didn't like him so he left. His boss burst out laughing while I stared aghast at my proud child.

'Talya! That wasn't your place to say that. I was going to tell him tonight myself.'

'Well, now you don't have to. Can I have another ice-cream?'

A half-hour passed and there was no sign of him. His boss went to see if he had fallen down the toilet, but he wasn't there. There was nothing else to do except pay the bill and leave. We found him outside the restaurant, sitting on the street, looking very dejected. He was broken-hearted. I felt awful, but what could I do?

This wasn't even an isolated incident. An Indian guy proposed to me in McDonalds after his mother gave her permission for him to do so—I had had one conversation with him the previous year. The only comfort I have is the fact that I'm getting older and Thai men prefer younger women. In fact, Thailand is a good place to age; there is a lot more respect for the older generation and I certainly see the difference in peoples' reactions to me now that I'm in my 40s. They take me a lot more seriously.

I miss the clean streets in America. More often than not I have to step around dead dogs on the crowded streets of the area in which I live, not to mention the frequent 'hills' of dog poop. My Thai friends laugh when I describe how Americans have to pick up their pet's poop and deposit it in the nearest bin. I miss the decent second-hand clothes shops, good internet connections, friendly policemen, cheap health food, ocean walks and the changing colours of the season. What I don't miss is the ridiculously huge food portions served in restaurants, the lack of global awareness, the chasing of the materialistic American dream and the fact that most people prefer to drive to a shop, or a friend's house, in the next street instead of walking to it.

***

While I was still in America I began to form an idea of what I wanted to focus on when I returned to Thailand. It started as a little nub in my brain and then grew the more I thought about it, and it was so obvious to me; I wanted to work with women. I had gone through so much in my life—falling in love, giving birth, single parenthood and being dramatically dumped at my lowest point physically, when I couldn't even get to the bathroom without help. I couldn't possibly let all these precious experiences go to waste. So, after Talya and I returned to Thailand I got involved with a well-established shelter for women. It is located in a beautiful part of Bangkok, and I had known about it for several years. It was set up by a nun who was released by her husband to follow her vocation. She had cancer and pleaded for her freedom to do this one thing while she still could. Fortunately, her husband was an understanding man and didn't stand in her way.

I actually met her 15 years ago when Nina and I visited the shelter to perform our 'box skit'. We had devised a way to catch young people's attention. Nina would narrate while I mimed the story of my life which would finish on a high note—that, at the end of the day, love was all that mattered. Coincidentally enough, Nina and I were invited back on Mother's Day this year and we performed the exact same skit to great results, 15 years later.

The shelter is a safe place for women who have been raped, or who have been driven to take their kids and flee abusive husbands, or have been infected with HIV, or who are pregnant and alone. I love working there. With my prison projects things could get quite difficult as I was constantly hearing about people dying, or dealing with men who were going to spend the rest of their lives behind bars. Remember my friend Dtui who had so much to give and ending up contracting HIV in Bang Kwang, which ultimately robbed him of the chance to turn around his life? He died so young, it just wasn't fair. This kind of work can become quite depressing as you can imagine. So, there is no better antidote than looking after pregnant women and then helping them to take care of their babies. The shelter is all about life!

Don't get me wrong, it's not Heaven. Some of these girls have done the most dreadful things to try and abort their babies, but the babies survive and come out fighting. Other girls are unceremoniously dumped here by their families. I was telling this to another Thai woman recently and she thought I was making it up. She couldn't believe that a Thai could ever dump their pregnant daughter and not want to have anything to do with their grandchildren.

'Are you kidding?' I replied, 'It happens all the time, and not only in Thailand.'

I found it really interesting to discover how many women were there because they didn't want their parents to know they were pregnant, and I'm not talking about young teenagers, I'm talking about women in their 20s and 30s whose self-esteem is fragile and are still very much afraid of letting down their parents.

I first started with giving a three month course to pregnant girls in which I taught them all about giving birth and the aftermath—how to take care of their nipples, their vaginas, how to breast-feed and care for their bundles of joy. Once I proved myself with this course I would be free to come and go and do what I wanted within the shelter. Technically, it was an excellent course but I felt something was missing. There didn't appear to be any real connection between me and the girls. Some of them had become pregnant after rape and others had been abandoned as a result of their pregnancy so they were pretty much a damaged lot. I worried that they had too much respect for me as a *farang* teacher—which is a particular Thai trait—and this impeded their being able to fully relax in my company. I resolved to fix this.

One day after we had performed some floor exercises I asked the girls to sit up for a special meditation. They closed their eyes obediently and listened to me as I told them about the past few years of my life. I didn't hold back. I told them

I was adopted after being rejected by my birth mother, that I did drugs and alcohol, that my teenage boyfriend had broken my nose, that I had loved and had a child for a man I didn't marry, that I was a single mother, wanted to help people, and of course the whole story of Garth and our subsequent break-up. The girls couldn't believe what I was telling them. They couldn't believe that they could so closely relate to a white *farang*'s experience.

It was worth it—it pushed our relationship to a whole new level. I wasn't some perfect white lady coming in to talk down to them about their mistakes in life; I had gone through much of what they had and, as a result, I probably understood them better than most. It was a huge breakthrough. I even managed to get them to pose like a pregnant Demi Moore on the cover of *Vanity Fair* magazine. They weren't naked, but it was a big deal for them to allow me to take photos of their swollen bellies. They saw me now as one of them, just as I had become one of the 'banana brigade' at Bang Kwang when I embarked on a relationship with an inmate.

I always find it beneficial to point out how important mothers are in any society. Without mothers there would be no king, no politicians, no anyone. The girls really responded visually when I reminded them that mothers were responsible for shaping the future. Of course, we don't work pure miracles. Some girls have their babies and then take off, leaving the unwanted child behind. Others are too anxious to get on with their lives and leave the shelter too early, sometimes doing a runner in the middle of the night, only to return again with an unwanted pregnancy.

There is a lot of laughter at the shelter, courtesy of the women. The HIV women live in the building to the rear of the property. They used to be more segregated back in the early days when not a lot was known or understood about HIV. Thankfully things have greatly improved since and there is quite a good atmosphere of hope and strength. I had dinner in the canteen last week with three women who are HIV positive. Mae is from Chiangmai and always wears her hair in a tight pony-tail. Her body has been ravaged by the disease and she has few teeth left. Yet she is always smiling despite her circumstances. She contracted HIV from her unfaithful husband. She gave birth to a boy 13 years ago and thankfully knew not to breastfeed him so he was never infected with the virus. She was forced to leave the baby at a temple in Chonburi because there was no way she could support him, and she also had no way of knowing when the virus would claim her.

Today, he is a young monk. She proudly showed me photographs of him over dinner one evening. She was quite a gentlewoman, dressed in a pristine white blouse and dark skirt and looked like she had never had a bad word to say about anyone. Except, that is, for her husband.

'I'm only here because of my cheating husband. He brought it home to me. Men are bastards!'

Then she giggled and put her hand to her mouth for using such a terrible word. Calling someone a bastard is one of the worst insults in Thailand. Her companions giggled with her in appreciation.

Rena also picked up the virus from her husband. She came down with a fever and took herself to the hospital because she didn't know what was wrong with her. The doctor took a blood test as standard procedure and that is how she found out she was HIV positive. She has only recently been diagnosed, at the age of 45, and I don't think it has truly hit home yet. The eldest one of the three still looks relatively healthy. Her long hair is dyed a chestnut-brown, but I can see her roots. She told me that when she was first diagnosed she consumed handfuls of pills and now she only takes a couple a day.

On another visit I made with my friend Marie, we met another woman, who was also infected by her husband. She had done a bit of research on the subject of HIV and explained to me that the choice of medication available to the women at the house comes down to financial means. They can go on a course of 1,000 baht or 5,000 baht—naturally, there are less side effects with the more expensive course.

She was in poor condition on her arrival at the house. Her blood count was only 50 before she went on medication and then it took her a couple of weeks to deal with the side effects, which ranged from fevers and unsightly rashes to severe nausea. We laughed when she told us that long term effects can lead to an increase in the size of the breasts and a decrease in the size of the bottom. We told her that many women throughout the western world would be envious of such a figure! She smiled at the idea; I was afraid I had gone too far, like the time I told a class of (single) mothers-to-be that they couldn't be embarrassed about discussing their vaginas since they were all sexy mamas—which was why they were pregnant in the first place! However, they, like this particular woman, laughed as loudly as I did.

I asked her how she found out that she had the disease. She told me that it wasn't until the disease had spread to her eyes; she was gradually losing her sight when she went to the ophthalmologist who did lots of tests to find the cause of the problem. Eventually she was diagnosed and immediately packed herself off to the shelter. Amazingly she harbours no ill will against her husband and has decided, instead, that the disease has presented her with an opportunity to help others. She helps the staff out by nursing other patients who are worse off than her and she also attends the HIV support groups, which are held every two to three months. She says the meetings give her hope to continue fighting her condition and are a source of inspiration to her. She really believes that she will survive to help others and this keeps her going. She receives a wage from the shelter for the work she does and she puts it carefully aside for her kids' education. New arrivals are welcomed personally by her and she is always available to listen and give advice. These marvellously strong women have so much to give and teach. I am honoured to know them.

I had spent the last year trying not to be angry at Garth for the callous way he ended things. I think I was afraid that if I acknowledged my anger it would consume me and destroy my chances for a normal future. Now I realise that it's ok to get angry. In fact, it's healthy to get angry when someone has treated you so badly. It's all part of the process; you grieve, you get angry and most importantly you learn to forgive; only then can you begin to heal. These women have had to pick themselves up after their initial rage and they are determined to get some good out of the rest of the lives; whatever amount of time they have left, they are not going to waste it in being angry at what has happened.

There are also lots of children in the shelter and again some of them have had to see or deal with things that they shouldn't have. The worst thing is when they think the behaviour they have witnessed from their role models is the proper code of conduct. Mith is an 11-year-old boy I got to know here. His mother had taken him and his sister and sneaked away from the family home. For years Mith watched his alcoholic father beat up his mother and it was a perfectly normal occurrence as far as he was concerned. He had an unhealthy attachment to his father and thought he could do no wrong—this is normal with abusive parents. Anyway, he had learned how to treat women from his father so when he arrived into this community of women he started to strike out. His language was foul, courtesy of his father, and he demanded constant attention. He was very angry at being separated from his father and never missed an opportunity to express it.

Unfortunately, he was the eldest of the children in the shelter which gave him power over them. Fortunately, however, the women understood the reasons behind his violent temper and worked together to gently admonish and encourage him to control himself. Then the little family took off for a while and I didn't see him. It turned out that Mith had a complete breakdown and ended up in the children's ward of the mental hospital where he received medication and anger counselling. I got a shock when I saw him again; he was terribly skinny.

I am working closely with him today. I discovered that he loves to massage people's shoulders and hands; he used to do this for his father. This is a very positive thing as it means that he can happily massage me while I give a class or counselling session; before, he used to resent me talking to another person when he was with me and I wasn't sure how to deal with it. Encouragement and compliments are always a balm for troubled children.

When Mith massages anyone they always take care to tell him how good he is at massaging and how strong he must be and so forth. It works wonders. Next year Mith will be ready to attend school with the other kids. In the meantime, his mother is studying so that she can get a good job to support her kids.

***

Here I am now back in Thailand amongst old friends and places. I am so glad that I made it here in one piece. This time last year I wasn't so sure. This book has been a huge healing process, seeing me going through umpteen journals and re-reading hundreds of emails and letters. I had to go right back to the beginning and start again, with hindsight, a humbling experience indeed. I have been incredibly fortunate. For 30 years or more I have lived out of a suitcase. At first it was on account of all the travelling I was doing but then, over time, it became a comfort to know that I was ready to move immediately if I had to.

In America, I did unpack for a while and it made me edgy and uncomfortable, especially when things began to go wrong. I am glad to write today that my suitcase is empty and is buried under my bed. I am more at peace now here in my little house on the edge of Bangkok than I have been in a long, long while. Apart from wishing that Thailand did a proper celebration of Christmas I don't want for anything else at this moment in time. (Although a few of us are organising a Christmas/New Year party at Bang Kwang which will be as enjoyable for me as it will be for the 200 inmates and prison officers.) My daughter survived the perils of the last few years with me and I now want to focus on her future. I am still doing some work in the prison, reluctantly retaining my title as the name of this book suggests, but much less than before, because I want to focus my energies on her and elsewhere. It is time to close the book on the past.

Friends ask me why I don't get rid of my 'Garth stuff'. I'm not a collector but I have kept his letters, in plastic folders, in chronological order! Maybe one day I'll throw them out but, for now, I like knowing that they are here. Some of them are incredibly beautiful and were meant at the time.

Through personal hard work and the power of forgiveness, my anger has abated, allowing me to finally move on. My days are as full as ever; visiting the women's shelter, Bang Kwang, the drug rehab centres and the slums.

I love what I do. It has been my life's work and I will continue to do it with wrinkles and aging limbs. I still have my bad days—I'm only human, and there is the constant tussle between the scars and the blessings. It's hard to get the balance just right.

There is a Sigmund Freud quote that means a lot to me; it sums up what I feel is the essence of life, and is an apt way to finish off my story; *One day, in retrospect, the years of struggle will strike you as the most beautiful.*

I hope that through my work I can share this sentiment of hope to those I try to help.

AFTERWORD

I remember the contradictory emotions I felt about my mother while growing up. People were constantly praising her for her accomplishments, constantly interested in her life story, and almost always finding themselves bewitched by this 5ft 6" spunky, down to earth, blonde bombshell. They were almost always telling me what a jewel she was and how I should aspire to be half the woman she is when I grew up.

I suppose I was more than a little confused how my mother—*my mother*—who laughs hideously loudly, cried hysterically over dying her hair the wrong colour, gets pimples, bad haircuts, and sometimes suffers from horrific black moods, could be portrayed as the 'Angel of Bang Kwang'; a saint who roams some of the filthiest maximum security prisons, slums, wards etc., yet always seems to emerge pure and untouched, and smiling. I thought, 'Shit, I want a refund because this isn't exactly an accurate perception of the mother I know.'

The mother I knew was bouncy and full of energy, temperamental, yet always as compensatory with her affectionate mannerisms. My mother is a classic example of a strong woman, a real woman, because, of course, she is not perfect and she is not a saint and no, she does not flitter above us all with perfumed farts and angelic melodies to thrill all who suffer. In fact, she's tone deaf and a terrible singer. But, she does try her damnedest to make a difference and she does genuinely care about other people. She is the most unselfish being I know—most of the time she is so consumed in helping others that she would forget to take care of herself. Sometimes I've wondered who is the parent as, occasionally, I've had to remind her to eat, remind her to run and pay the bills, make her cups of tea and comfort her when she bursts into tears of frustration and exhaustion.

Yet, when it comes right down to it, she has never been lackadaisical in providing me with a healthy, stable home—sometimes going without so that I wouldn't miss out. She also never made me feel like I had to hide anything from her, which I did anyway. I've discovered since then that honesty is always the best policy when dealing with her. And I am eternally grateful that I always had, and have, both such a cool friend to confide in and a mother's wisdom to guide me through the tribulations of childhood and everything that prepubescent ignorance brought me. Thanks to her open and unconditionally accepting attitude I had a safeguard to keep me from ever really falling off the ledge.

Not that she had all the answers, far from it, but who does? She has had to deal with the heartache of being both father and mother to me, which I greatly resented because she had to be both the disciplinary guardian and the loving, caring one too—which made her appear hypocritical in my young eyes.

Sometimes we got along like Siamese twins, skipping out on my school work to go to a movie, having hot cocoa, dancing hysterically around the living room, taking long walks; listening to her mad stories about her experiences and her defending me against my evil grade-school teacher who made my life a living hell. Then, around the time our hormones started to wax and wane, we fought like rabid hyenas on steroids. Sometimes, I was tempted to feel a little neglected, what with her busy schedule and jailbird love.

At other times, she seemed detached and too preoccupied to focus on me, which gave me ample time get into mischief. However, her approach as I got older was to give me independence and the freedom to make mistakes and learn from them by myself, while she stood on the sidelines watching me carefully, which was a double-edged sword because I was still a child and should have been wrapped up in protective layers, and coddled and cossetted, and not trusted to have the maturity to decipher between right and wrong.

However, it was, in hindsight, the right method for me because, though I fell, I learnt how to deal with it. I learnt from my wrongs and benefited from my rights and I became strong at the art of coping, just like she is.

And at the end of the day, I doubt that there will ever be someone who loves me as unconditionally as my mom.

- Talya Lindsey Hattan, 2007

MORE NON-FICTION FROM MAVERICK HOUSE

THE LAST EXECUTIONER

MEMOIRS OF THAILAND'S LAST PRISON EXECUTIONER

BY CHAVORET JARUBOON
WITH NICOLA PIERCE

Chavoret Jaruboon was personally responsible for executing 55 prison inmates on Thailand's infamous death row.

As a boy, he wanted to be a teacher like his father, then a rock'n'roll star like Elvis, but his life changed when he joined Thailand's prison service. From there he took on one of the hardest jobs in the world.

Honest and often disturbing—but told with surprising humour and emotion—*The Last Executioner* is the remarkable story of one man's experiences with life and death.

Emotional and at times confronting, the book grapples with the controversial topic of the death sentence and makes no easy reading.

This book is not for the faint hearted—*The Last Executioner* takes you right behind the bars of the Bangkok Hilton and into death row.

To order this book go to www.maverickhouse.com

MORE NON-FICTION FROM MAVERICK HOUSE

WELCOME TO HELL

One Man's Fight for Life inside
the 'Bangkok Hilton'

By COLIN MARTIN

Written from his cell and smuggled out page by page,
Colin Martin's autobiography chronicles an innocent man's
struggle to survive inside one of the world's most dangerous
prisons.

After being swindled out of a fortune, Martin was let down
by the hopelessly corrupt Thai police. Forced to rely upon
his own resources, he tracked down the man who conned
him and, drawn into a fight, accidentally stabbed and killed
the man's bodyguard.

Martin was arrested, denied a fair trial, convicted of murder
and thrown into prison—where he remained for eight
years. Honest and often disturbing, *Welcome to Hell* is the
remarkable story of how Martin was denied justice again
and again.

In his extraordinary account, he describes the swindle, his
arrest and vicious torture by police, the unfair trial, and
the eight years of brutality and squalor he was forced to
endure.

To order this book go to www.maverickhouse.com